D0896377

BASIC
EVANGELISM

BASIC EVANGELISM

by

C. E. AUTREY

PROFESSOR OF EVANGELISM
New Orleans Baptist Theological Seminary

**ZONDERVAN
PUBLISHING HOUSE** OF THE ZONDERVAN CORPORATION
GRAND RAPIDS, MICHIGAN 49506

Basic Evangelism
Copyright 1959 by
Zondervan Publishing House
Grand Rapids, Michigan

Thirteenth printing December 1975

Printed in the United States of America

To
my wife
ALINE HILTON AUTREY
and sons
JARRY *and* CARROL

FOREWORD

To measure the full dimensions of a book it needs to be seen in its total context. The framework of this volume is found in an institution that from its beginning has made a unique and distinct contribution to the spread of the Gospel in the name of evangelism.

When Dr. L. R. Scarborough left his pastorate at the great First Baptist Church in Abilene to come to the new seminary in Waco, he brought to the foundation of the seminary a "hot heart." His ministry had been signally favored of God in evangelism. He was a very personal soul-winner. In this new institution he established the "Chair of Fire," which has been a distinguishing flame in the earth wherever Southwestern is mentioned. It is not that he discovered evangelism at Southwestern, for that is the common property of all disciples of Jesus; but at Southwestern Dr. Scarborough gave to evangelism an organic articulation which became a kindling flame in Southern Baptist life.

When Dr. C. E. Autrey came to the Seminary in 1955 to occupy the Chair of Evangelism, he came in the maturity of an evangelistic ministry. His pastorates had been permeated with personal witnessing and evangelistic preaching. He had served as a state leader of evangelism and then as a member of the staff of the Home Mission Board Department of Evangelism. His had been a vital part in the formulation of our present Southern Baptist program of evangelism. Academically, his doctoral studies had been in the field of the Greek New Testament.

Already he has placed the mark of his evangelistic spirit upon the Seminary. He has entered into the mainstream of its witness and made contribution to it. His classes are inspirational as well as informational.

It is fitting that his first book, born in this atmosphere, should be one entitled "Basic Evangelism." Evangelism itself is basic. All that we do as disciples of Jesus must have evangelistic content. The end purpose of all Christian witnessing and activities is evangelism. But here that which is primary is divided into its basic parts. The "what it is" and "how it is to be done" are met together in this single volume.

It is a happy privilege to commend the author to the reader and the book to its multiple purposes. It will be a textbook of genuine worth in our colleges and seminaries. It will be an encouragement to every hungry-hearted pastor desiring to be more effective in his witness. Basic evangelism is just that which its title implies: the foundation principles for the seeking of the lost multitudes.

ROBERT E. NAYLOR,
President, Southwestern
Theological Seminary

Fort Worth, Texas
September, 1959

CONTENTS

BASIC
EVANGELISM

Chapter 1

THE THEOLOGICAL BASIS OF EVANGELISM

Evangelism and theology are complementary to each other and utterly dependent upon each other. The heart of the Gospel of the New Testament is theological. Theology and evangelism are therefore relevant. There has been for some time the mistaken notion that there is a kind of antithesis between theology and evangelism. Some theologians look with suspicion upon evangelism, and many evangelists avoid theology. The theologian may consider evangelism as shallow and over-emotional. Some evangelism has been shallow and given to disgraceful excesses, but that is not the fault of true evangelism. Some theologians are cold, impractical, and dull, but that cannot be charged to theology. There can be no effective and permanent evangelism without theology, and there would soon be few persons ready to study theology without evangelism.

EVANGELISM AND THEOLOGY COMPLEMENT EACH OTHER

The leading evangelists of each generation have considered theology a help rather than a hindrance.

1. Paul was a mighty theologian. He gave us Christianity in its doctrinal expressions. God poured through Paul's brains germinal doctrines which became mighty material in the hands of Augustine and Calvin. The great depth and range of thought, exemplified in the Epistles to the Romans, Ephesians, Titus, and others, cause modern theologians to marvel. His thinking ability and profound theological grasp did not circumscribe his evangelistic fervor. He was a great evangelist, and it was theology that formed the basis of his powerful message. He burned himself out in the field of evangelism, and he pressed hard to adequately present Christ to a confused world. His world was largely confused because of its lack of clear thinking. Paul never could have

13

reached the minds and hearts of his generation so completely without much study and clear, convincing thinking.

2. Augustine was a great theologian. He formulated the theology which Luther and his contemporaries so effectively used many centuries later in the Reformation. Augustine was an effective evangelist. He did not use the methods of modern evangelists. He did not go about holding two-week revivals in local churches, nor did he conduct a single city-wide campaign; yet he formulated the revealed truth of Christianity into convicting and burning expressions which moved men Godward. The same thing can be said of Calvin. Evangelism will never be able to pay its debt to these two great theologians.

3. Jonathan Edwards was the greatest Christian scholar in America in the first half of the eighteenth century. He was an outstanding theologian. He was recognized as an authority in theology, both in America and England. History records that the Great Awakening really had its beginning in his church in 1734. He was one of the three leading evangelists in the Awakening which turned the colonies back to God. Edwards, Whitefield, and Gilbert Tennent were followers of Calvin.

After the fires of the Awakening died down, a group of hyper-Calvinists gradually came into position and all but completely smothered the flame of evangelism.

4. Charles G. Finney taught systematic theology in Oberlin College for over forty years. He was the most effective evangelist of his generation. His great grasp of theology greatly enhanced his message.

Theology often produces revival, and revival greatly strengthens theology. New theological emphases have often generated revival. Finney turned from hyper-Calvinism to place emphasis on human responsibility in salvation. Finney held that revival is not a miracle. He defines a miracle "as a divine interference, setting aside or suspending the laws of nature." He said in explanation, "there is nothing in religion beyond the ordinary powers of nature." Finney made these statements to counter the prevailing views of the hyper-Calvinists. They held that God is sovereign and will give revival to the world and salvation to men when it pleases Him to do so. They held that revivals are not to be promoted, and God saves whomsoever He chooses without human agencies. They also believed that revival came every five or twenty-five years, or only when God saw fit to send it on inactive and unexpectant churches. Charles Finney sought to impress upon his generation that men are accountable before God and that lost men have a responsibility for their salvation. He held that if lost men, drawn by the Holy Spirit, came to Christ, they could be saved.

We believe that both Finney and his Calvinistic contemporaries went to extremes which could have been avoided. We cannot agree with Finney that "there is nothing in religion beyond the ordinary powers of nature."[1] Souls cannot be saved and no revival winds can blow without the presence and work of the Holy Spirit. The powerful work of the Holy Spirit is beyond the "ordinary powers of nature." Finney gave his emphasis to urge churches to adopt "new measures" in promoting revivals. In spite of these extreme statements, God was able to use the new theological emphasis to move men in great revival proportions.

Apart from the use of prayer and other measures, some overlooked or otherwise dormant theological truth has frequently been used to give biblical weight and drive to every great revival. In the Reformation it was "salvation by grace." In the Wesleyan revival it was the "new birth." In the western revival the conscience was awakened to the great theological truth that all men are accountable before God and are responsible to co-operate with God in repentance and faith to receive salvation.

EVANGELISM DEPENDS UPON THEOLOGY

1. The purpose of theology is to define and explain our Evangel. Evangelism presents and applies the evangelical portion of our message. Furthermore, evangelism furnishes the desire to master every ramification of our Evangel. The evangelist confronts the lost world with evangelical truth and urges it upon those who hear. This truth must be defined and made meaningful. At this vital point, evangelism is utterly dependent upon theology. An unrelated, confused, or vague message, however energetically presented, will fail to gain the attention and respect of the listening world.

2. Evangelism is the living expression of doctrinal theology. Evangelism is not to be defined as a mere branch of practical

theology. It is not founded upon isolated texts, concepts, and practices, but upon the total meaning of the Christian faith.

It is time to face some probing questions; such as, Does our program of evangelism grow out of American activism or out of the Gospel? Have we been beguiled into taking our ever increasing church membership as a criterion of spiritual advance? It is true that many of our churches are beehives of activity and some of them of highly organized activity, but does this movement spell out evangelistic aggrandizement? Such questions raise the issue of whether evangelism has an adequate theological foundation.

We must make sure that our evangelism does not draw upon a bag of clever tricks. It must draw upon the very truth by which the church lives and moves and has its being.[2] We must slay all tricks, traps, and techniques which will cheapen evangelism. In Asia they recently asked a teacher as he tried to teach evangelism to the pastors in conference, "Are your methods scriptural?" "Do these techniques grow out of the truth or are they gimmicks?" They were asking him, "Does your evangelism have a theological basis?" Evangelism, in the present as in the past, could easily become an outgrowth of pragmatism devoid of the basic truths of the Bible. This cannot happen if our evangelism is kept properly related to theology.

Theology is to evangelism what the skeleton is to the body. Remove the skeleton and the body becomes a helpless quivering mass of jelly-like substance. By means of the skeleton the body can stand erect and move. The great system of theological truths forms the skeleton which enables our revealed religion to stand.

THE AIMS OF EVANGELISM

1. The first aim of evangelism is to confront the world with the Gospel of Christ. To do this effectively one must have an intellectual grasp of the Gospel. One of the greatest problems of evangelism relates to the intellectual. The moral problem often eclipses the intellectual in our consideration, but this often makes for ineffective evangelization. In our day everything is being questioned, and thinking men demand clearly expressed answers. The aim of evangelism now is not to emote, but to promote. There might have been a time when theatrical and emotional

appeals would have sufficed, but not so today. The evangelism that will prove helpful now must be undergirded by a sound and sane theology.[3]

2. The second aim of evangelism is to secure clear and definite decisions to accept Christ as Saviour and. to enlist all converts as effective followers of Christ. When this aim is achieved, it is through effective confrontation. In accomplishing the goal of effective confrontation, theology is a necessity. A careful knowledge and understanding of theology contributes to effective evangelism in two ways: theology helps make the Evangel simple, and it is an agent in conserving results.

(a) A knowledge of theology helps to make our gospel message plain. We speak of God only because He has spoken to us. God reaches down to men. Men do not unveil God. Christianity is a revealed religion. Luther said that it was foolish to talk about God in personal terms unless we have experienced God. God must precede our idea of God. God remains an empty abstraction unless we actually meet Him personally. This experience is called faith.

In the seventh chapter of John when Jesus attended the Feast of Tabernacles, He faced a critical group[4] who inquired of Him, "How do you know you are really talking about God and not merely voicing an opinion concerning Him?" Jesus replied, "If any man will do his will, he shall know of the doctrine, whether it be of God, or whether I speak of myself" (John 7:17). The answer of Jesus revealed that knowledge of God is not theoretical. It is a matter of the whole personality confronting God and living out the implications of the encounter. This statement teaches us that Christian truth is more than revealed truth. It is redemptive also. It is more than a communication of ideas; it is a transmission of divine power. When one brings the knowledge to men that they can have newness of life and can know that their sins are forgiven, then leads them into this experience, he evangelizes.

The great doctrines, such as those of the judgment, sin, atonement, repentance, faith, justification, Christ, the resurrection, and others, make up our theology. When they are fully and intelligently presented, they will make our message relevant and appealing. Every great truth must be presented in the light of all the truths. If this is done, our message will be consistent, acceptable, and simple. To tear a few words out of their context and present them as a full-orbed facet of the truth is often contradictory and confusing. Anyone who has a well-rounded knowledge of the Scriptures will avoid this practice as if it were a poison adder.

There is no such thing as making the Gospel simple unless one has been down among the deep and profound things of God until they become a part of him. What we too often define as simplicity is nothing more than shallow, foamy beating of the air. The study of theology helps to clarify one's own thoughts and produces a clear understanding of what the Gospel means for him. When one can apply the gospel Evangel to himself, he can effectively apply it to the needs of others. The more one knows, the more likely he is to be simple in his interpretation. Generally a man is obscure because he has never understood his material and has never come to grips with his problems.

(b)   Theology is an agent in conserving evangelistic results. This is another way in which a knowledge of theology contributes to effective evangelism. The superficial evangelist will overlook this vital fact. The evangelism that stops with saving the soul and does not go on to build Christian character is inadequate. Evangelism's greatest failure is found in the fact that too many converts do not stand. They soon fade from the picture because their knowledge of the faith is so inadequate. Evangelism's chief problem is to hold its converts and enlist them in the total ministry of the church. Christian character is a basic essential. The only way to build Christian character is through a steady diet of the strong meat of the Word. A thorough spiritual diet of doctrinal instruction can grow bones and muscles of Christian character. All other efforts to enlist and conserve evangelistic results will fail if this basic truth is ignored.

Converts who are taught the great doctrines of our faith will know what they believe, why they believe it, and that they should be faithful to it (Rom. 5:2). They will not be upset by every wind that blows, and they will become strong soldiers in the army of Christ (Eph. 4:14).

Jesus was a popular preacher, but He saw the futility of merely spraying the multitudes with the Gospel. He selected twelve men and gave most of His energy to instructing them with His doctrines. He imbued them with His spirit so He could leave the church to their safe leadership when His work was done.[5] He often poured out His soul to the crowds when the opportunity came, but He majored on instructing the disciples.

Francis Xavier in the fifteenth century traveled further and went to more lands to evangelize than any missionary before him. He went as far away as Japan. He sprayed the crowds with the Gospel and sprinkled them with holy water; but when he passed on, his evangelism faded away. Very little spiritual fruit remained to show that he had ever lived. When Hudson Taylor went to China, the multitudes flocked to hear him preach and many responded, but at the end of the year there was little gain in church membership to show for this great preaching to mighty multitudes. Then Taylor returned from the crowds and set up a church in a small hut. He began to give his attention to instructing thoroughly the few real converts so that through strong Christian Chinese men and women he could reach the masses. When he did this, he had more permanent results. He had learned the technique of Jesus.

INADEQUATE THEOLOGY CURBS EVANGELISM

There are several intellectual deflections which have affected the theology of evangelism over the last fifty years. Generally the preponderance of writing and teaching in these directions has diluted the stream of theological thought and in turn sapped evangelistic vitality.

An inadequate theology based on humanism and naturalistic psychology undermines the main thrust of evangelism. A knowledge of psychology and science is helpful. The preponderance of writing in the field of psychology and science has been invigorating and helpful to religion. All psychology and science therefore is not bad but, on the contrary, has been very helpful. It must be pointed out, however, that any theology which is based solely on natural explanations and insights is inadequate as a basis of evangelism.

1.   Humanistic theology is inadequate because it neglects the evidence of God's self-revelation. Theistic naturalism believes in the reality of God but denies the existence of a personal God. To some, God is no more than the behavior of the universe.[6] The theistic naturalist denies the supernatural. His limited conception of God leads to such a conclusion. Anyone who believes

in a personal God will have no difficulty accepting the supernatural. "Supernaturalism is no mere recrudescence of prescien-
tific lore."[7]

2. Naturalistic psychology has subtly poisoned the currents
of theological thought. As we have already pointed out, psychology has a place and as a science is important. It cannot and
will not be brushed aside as irrelevant by men with a thorough
grasp of this field of human need. We are here concerned with
only one phase of psychology. We only point out the dangerous
implications involved in naturalistic psychology.

Much of the naturalistic psychology in our century stems
from behaviorism. Behavioristic psychology would explain all
human action in physiological terms.[8] Most of the early be-
haviorists were not necessarily materialistic, for they believed
that mind was not a form of matter.[9] Naturalistic psychology
accepts the fact of consciousness but declares that if superhuman
factors were operative in consciousness, psychology would be
able to discover them.[10] Naturalistic psychology holds that this
sort of evidence cannot be found in the human experience.
Therefore, the whole idea of the new birth is laughed out of
school by this group.

Naturalistic psychology regards conversion as perfectly ex-
plicable by the laws of psychology. No divine agent is involved,
they declare. However, we must remember that psychology is a
science. Science knows nothing of the subjective and has no
knowledge of the relations that lie behind the experience of a
soul.[11] Psychology as a science is only concerned with what it
observes. Its function is to describe what it observes. Religious
psychology cannot concern itself with the reality within us
known as the soul. It cannot observe the soul. Christianity is
more than subjective. There is a place for religious psychology,
but the purpose of religious psychology is not to explain conversion. Conversion is the work of the Holy Spirit.

3. How have these intellectual deflections affected evangelism in the last fifty years?

(1) Humanism depersonalized God and robbed us of the
power of God. A preacher must believe in the living God, must
believe in His presence, and must feel that he has a mission
from God. He must feel that he is an instrument in the hands of
God and under the guidance of the Supreme Being, or he will be

spiritually impotent. Theistic humanism blurred the truth concerning the supernatural and in many quarters has broken down the spirit to meet the challenge of the apparently impossible. It took away the drive of faith so vital to the evangelist and replaced it with mental calculations in the realm of speculation.

(2)   Naturalistic psychology distorts the modern conception of conversion. It asserts that there is no phenomenon of religious life which cannot be explained by psychophysical laws. It describes conversion as an emotional crisis which is not the result of an experience with God but which grows out of an accumulation of experiences and circumstances within the life of the convert.

A VITAL THEOLOGY OF EVANGELISM

We shall not give an exhaustive study to the theology of evangelism. We shall not attempt to cover every phase of it. We shall only take up two or three of its most vital points.

1.   Sin and salvation. The term "salvation" in this discussion is used to designate the initial experience of the sinner's deliverance from the dominion of sin. Redemption comes from God. It never originates with man. Man must want this salvation and must accept it on God's terms. Sin ruined man. Man was in a hopeless state. God initiated a plan of grace through which man could be reconciled to God (Eph. 2:8). God entered history by the Incarnation. He took upon Himself the nature of man and in man's nature offered a sacrifice which made it possible for Him to forgive sinful man and remain just (Phil. 2:5-11). "Salvation is not a matter of laws and regulations, ceremonies and institutions . . . it is a redemptive fellowship between a personal God and a personal man."[12] The unredeemed are under the tyranny of spiritual darkness with the devil on the throne. Through salvation the reign of Satan is broken. He is dethroned in the life of the redeemed sinner, and a new reign is inaugurated. Christ comes to rule the life. To have the reign of Satan overthrown in one's life is only half the work of salvation. Righteousness, peace, and good will must reign and Christ must occupy the throne. When Satan is cast out, Jesus comes in to rule and fill the life with positive goodness. Salvation is a spiritual revolution. A rule of terror is swept away and a reign of righteousness and joy

begins. The saved ceases to live in a negative state and becomes a force for positive good in the world.

Salvation is God's answer to the sin problem. Many so-called religious leaders claim that all man needs to do about sin is to rid himself of the burdensome idea of sin.[13] When man rids himself of the idea of sin, he will also remove the reality of sin. This school of thought holds that the worst thing about sin is the current notion of sin. Eliminate the idea of sin and one is free from sin. Such an argument is just another evidence of the blinding effect of sin on the mind. Bible-believing scholars have always recognized the reality of sin. Spiritually blind religionists have always denied the reality of sin. The Apostle John came to grips with the same problem in the early days of Christianity when he argued, "If we say that we have not sinned, we make him [God] a liar, and his word is not in us" (I John 1:10).

John Calvin held that sin is not an act.[14] Each act of sin only reflects a state. Sin is a state or a condition of the soul. Man does not become a sinner because of acts of sin, but he commits acts of sin because he is a sinner by nature. Man is totally depraved. Depravity does not mean that a man is as vile as possible, nor that all his acts are evil. The depraved man may satisfy most of the demands of the society in which he lives and be recognized as a good citizen. Total depravity means that all of man's nature is damaged by sin, and that he is ruled by sin. It means that man's relations with God are broken and that he cannot build an acceptable relationship with God by his deeds. Since sin is a state and since man is totally depraved, he cannot save himself from sin. No act, however good, can atone.[15] Man cannot even initiate reconciliation. He cannot make the first step toward God. God initiates reconciliation. This is what God does in the Incarnation and the Cross.[16] Many expressions are used in the Bible to portray the nature of man's salvation in Christ. The word "ransom" (Mark 10:45), and the expressions, "with a price" (I Cor. 6:20), "made sin" (II Cor. 5:21), and also "propitiation" for sin (Rom. 3:25), and many others set the bases for salvation.[17] These terms clearly teach that the death of Christ is essential to the salvation of sinners. The blood of Christ has cleansing effect on the believer (I John 1:7). Dr. Fred L. Fisher points out that the incarnation, death, and resurrection of Christ are not to be separated but that all three constitute God's redemptive move toward man.[18]

Through the Cross, God provides forgiveness. Often in our day, psychiatric therapy is substituted for forgiveness. Counseling has a great place in correcting twisted relations of human beings and bringing relief to individuals, but to seek to provide relief and comfort without removing the underlying cause of tensions is like taking aspirin to reduce the fever which will continue to recur until the disease is cured. The majority of the bedeviling tensions which plague humanity stem from a deep-seated consciousness of guilt. People with guilt complexes must be changed, and they must know that the wrongs have been corrected and absolved. A sense of real forgiveness is essential in human relations to bring permanent relief. Of course, we must remember that forgiveness of sin goes deeper than just removing the sense of guilt. Most of the fears, tensions, and disturbing factors which unhinge people today stem from the need of forgiveness from God. A fundamental wrongness prevails, and though the person may not always be able to analyze and locate its source, he is aware that it is present. What he needs is freedom from the burden which pulls him down. He can be free. He needs someone to patiently, yet frankly, confront him with the Gospel of forgiveness, based on the Cross.

The brothers of Joseph back in the Old Testament needed the spiritual therapy of forgiveness (Gen. 50:19-21). They had committed a grave injustice against their brother many years before. The feeling of guilt had, for the most part, been dormant until a personal crisis arose. The crisis produced a deep sense of guilt for past sins. Their sins came to the surface like a deadly submarine loaded with missiles of destruction. The feeling of guilt gave birth to fear. They sent a messenger to Joseph from their father, saying, "So shall ye say unto Joseph, Forgive, I pray thee now" (Gen. 50:17). They personally asked for forgiveness, and when Joseph heard them, he relieved their fears by assuring them that they had nothing to fear from him.

The people in the wilderness had sinned a great sin. Moses did not try to superficially relieve them of the guilt complex, but he went directly to God and pleaded, "Yet now, if thou wilt forgive their sin —; and if not, blot me, I pray thee, out of thy book which thou has written" (Exod. 32:32). They, like the brothers of Joseph, needed forgiveness. They needed to be restored to favor with God. Without the favor of God's presence they would perish. When they became aware of the magnitude of their sin and the significance of the withdrawal of God's presence, they truly repented and were forgiven. Without forgiveness their guilt would have destroyed them.

Personal contact with God is essential to forgiveness. "If we confess our sins, he is faithful and just to forgive us our sins, and to cleanse us from all unrighteousness" (I John 1:9). Forgiveness is preceded by an inward desire for justification. When this desire blooms into a confession to God, then God gladly exercises forgiveness. There will be no confession apart from repentance and faith. The next vital steps in the theology of evangelism, therefore, are repentance and faith.

2. Repentance and faith. Salvation is personal. Salvation is based therefore on a personal response.[19] "The necessary response may be described as a complete change of allegiance on man's part from sin to God and a trusting committal of self to God."[20] In this statement we have a definition of faith and repentance. In a life of sin, man's loyalties are misplaced. He is a citizen of a world foreign to the nature of God. Man in his natural world is committed to it and moves with the impulses of that world. God must come into man's world and get his personal response. We have seen how God by the incarnation, death, and resurrection of Christ has entered the world and offered man a new life. It now becomes man's responsibility to accept or reject. "By whom also we have access by faith into this grace wherein we stand, and rejoice in hope of the glory of God" (Rom. 5:2). "Therefore it is of faith, that it might be by grace" (Rom. 4:16). We have access to God's grace by faith only, and the response has to be faith that salvation might be by grace. Paul uses Abraham as an illustration of this axiom when he declared, "Abraham believed God, and it was counted unto him for righteousness. . . . He staggered not at the promise of God through unbelief; but was strong in faith. . . . And therefore it was imputed to him for righteousness" (Rom. 4:3, 20, 22). These Scriptures remind us that faith was not a new departure in God's relations to man. Faith was the necessary response even in the days of Abraham, centuries before the coming of God into history in the Incarnation.

Faith is confidence in God (Heb. 11:1). It is more than confidence. It is an experience with God which translates God from a mere concept into a vital, personal reality. Saving faith is a trustful surrender of one's entire being and destiny into the hands of God. Through this experience one becomes a son of God. "As many as received him, to them gave he power to become the sons of God, even to them that believe on his name" (John 1:13). Faith is confidence enough in God to take Him at His word and receive the gift of eternal life. "He that believeth on the Son hath everlasting life" (John 3:36).

Repentance, like faith, is a work of grace. No man can repent at will. God works repentance in man, but man must co-operate with God in the experience. When the Word of God and the Holy Spirit work a condition of repentance in the soul, then man is accountable for following through. Faith and repentance are inseparably tied together.

Decision means to end debate in favor of one side or the other.[21] It means to come to a conclusion that a certain thing is correct. One may be convinced that a proposition is right but never take action. Faith means to take a stand for the proposition. Repentance is a shift of life's emphases growing out of the experience of decision of faith. The repentant man possesses a disposition necessary for spiritual re-creation.[22] When one has faith and repentance, he leans toward God with an open heart and mind. He is no longer self-sufficient and filled with pride, but he is critical of self and dependent on God. When the sinner repents, he turns about-face and when he does, he looks God in the face. This is the bitterness of repentance. He has been running from God with his back to God. In repentance he faces God and sees then what he has suspected all along — the guilt and wrongness of his own life. But he also sees the real purpose of God in redemption. He sees that God does not point an accusing finger at him but is eager to forgive and restore him. He sees reflected in God's face the love of God. The bitterness of soul soon melts into a joy too deep to be put into words. The grace of God completes the work of repentance. Man responds to the goodness of God (Rom. 2:4). When the goodness of God leads to repentance, then God forgives sins; for repentance is the moral ground on which God forgives sins.[23]

Chapter 2

BIBLICAL BACKGROUND

Old Testament evangelism was largely a matter of revivals. There were no personal efforts on the part of anyone to win converts. It must also be remembered that Old Testament revivals were not revivals in the sense in which we think of revivals in modern times. They were not protracted meetings nor evangelistic crusades. They were periods of returning to God marked by spiritual fervor and repentance. The initial effort or activity often lasted only a day or a week, but results lived in the lives of the people for years. The history of Judah and Israel is replete with moral decline and spiritual revivals in unbroken sequence. These revival efforts were generally promoted by patriarchs, kings, scribes, and prophets of the Old Testament.

In the New Testament we find full-orbed evangelism. Jesus used both mass and personal evangelism. The apostles all followed the example of Jesus. Paul and many of the other apostles used writing, as well as mass and personal evangelism, to further spiritual conquest.

In order to get a clear understanding of the New Testament concept of evangelism, we must reject certain false impressions which are prevalent in our thinking about New Testament evangelism.

WHAT EVANGELISM IS NOT

1. Dr. Sweazey points out that some people think that evangelism is everything we do.[1] Often we do everything but evangelism. This definition is a far cry from the concept found in the New Testament. A church could use this kind of reasoning to excuse itself from every definite commission to which God has assigned it. It could say "everything we do is missions" and let the lost world outside of its immediate communion go on to eternity without a witness. This concept may be the reasoning

of a church member whose faith has never been defined in his own mind and whose experience is so vague it does not seem worth sharing with others. This view may be held by the Christian who has never learned how to present the plan of salvation to the lost. Evangelism is not everything we do. One might conceivably spend all his time doing good and never evangelize. Moral righteousness is not evangelism. One never evangelizes until he stands directly before the heart's door of a sinner and clearly confronts him with the Gospel of Christ.

2. Evangelism is not merely leading people to unite with the church. Too many of our present-day evangelistic meetings are no more than a drive for church membership. We are burning too much incense at the altar of numbers. We agree with Charles Spurgeon that those who never deal in numbers have no numbers to speak of, but there is a dangerous extreme.[2] This is an hour of commercialism. The spirit of this material age, if permitted to blast its way into our Christian concepts, will do irreparable harm. Instead of being faithful to the great body of revealed truth, declaring the Gospel with clarity and waiting on God to give results in deepening of conviction and spiritual life which is conducive to genuine conversion, we run ahead of God and begin pulling the fruit while it is still green. We just must have numbers. They must walk the aisles. We think it is imperative that we have more additions than during the previous effort. We, unawares, have begun judging revivals by a material standard. Spiritual values are never to be fitted into earthen molds. Those who are converted should be led to join the church, but church membership comes after conversion. There is an irresponsible evangelism today which knows little of real conversion and would hurriedly move on to place the premium on mere numbers and emotional excitement. This type must be curbed, or our churches may soon be filled with the unconverted. An unregenerate church membership is disastrous, regardless of how it becomes unregenerate. Before the Great Awakening the "halfway covenant" filled the churches with unregenerate people. We decry, but "numbers evangelism" will bring us to the same brink of disaster.

A healthy New Testament evangelism will add great numbers to our churches. But the goal of the evangelism of Jesus is the conversion of the individual, and not an ever lengthening church roll. Never decry numbers if numbers represent redeemed souls, but make sure your goal is to redeem rather than to count. An excellent test of evangelism is seen in its permanence. What happens several months after the method has been applied? Does church attendance increase? Do the Sunday School and Training Union show marked growth in spirit and interest? Is there a noticeable increase in power in the church, and does the church enjoy a period of permanent growth? Or, do things remain as before? True evangelism, whether it is in the form of revival or perennial emphasis, will look to the welfare of the evangelized and not necessarily to the names of the evangelists. It will enlist the converted into the total ministry of the church.

3.   Evangelism is not merely enlisting people in a new kind of activity. There are all kinds of clubs and organizations in our modern world. Most people belong to one or more of these organizations. People are busy. Most people, including many wives and mothers, work. People are in an inevitable whirl of endless activity. They could profitably use a little rest and quiet for mental reflection. There might be less juvenile thinking if people had less activity and more time for meditation. If our quest in evangelism is only to enlist folk in a new kind of activity, we shall have little to offer. Some of us are convinced that activity, even religious activity, is not the answer for our spiritually sick generation.

There is more activity now in one month in many of the churches of the great evangelical denominations than was expended by all denominations for the entire duration of any one of the great spiritual awakenings in the past. We could wish that all this activity were propelled by the Spirit of God. We, however, have grounds for fear that much of it is the contagion of a commercial age. Though we are numerically, financially, and culturally stronger, are we not also amazingly impotent? We must have more than impressive, outward appearance and physical power in our churches to impress our world and bring to it a conviction that it needs God. We must possess divine power. If we are to bring this world to God, we must have the same purpose and power which characterized the Early Church in the Book of Acts. They went out, not to enlist people in a certain type of activity, but to bear witness to an experience which they had with God. They told a simple story in the power of the Holy Spirit. The moving of the Holy Spirit was witnessed on every hand. As men were converted, they were added to the churches and became witnesses. The churches at Jerusalem, Antioch, and elsewhere became vigorous organizations full of life and activity, but activity was not an end in itself. They had one desire, and that was to preach Christ. They preached Christ and were convinced that the Holy Spirit would accomplish the work of salvation.

Their evangelism was a simple confrontation, nothing more. They confronted the pagan world with the news about Jesus, God's Son. They told what He had done for them. They told why He had been able to perfect the change in their lives. They called on men to repent and believe.

4. Evangelism is not a syncretism. It is not an effort at the coalescence of different forms of facts through accretions of tenets. There is a concerted effort in the "new evangelism" to syncretize. In foreign lands the new evangelism would seek to only Christianize Buddhism.[3] Just as Buddhism entered Japan centuries ago and merged with Shintoism, so would many evangelicals merge Christianity with whatever religion they find in the respective areas. This approach would not require the prospect to forsake his old communal relations nor to break drastically with any other religious ties which he may now hold dear. He would only pretend to live as a Christian. This approach is a departure from the method of the New Testament. The world which Paul faced is no different from that of our age. It was a time of race hatred, social discrimination, and moral indecency. Paul did not go to Asia Minor to work out a spiritual coalition with the pagan religions. He did not call for a weak allegiance, but for a complete loyalty to Christ.[4] He was not ashamed of the distinctiveness of his Gospel. He declared, "I am not ashamed of the gospel of Christ: for it is the power of God unto salvation to every one who believeth. . . . For therein is the righteousness of God revealed. . . . the wrath of God is revealed" (Rom. 1:16-18). Paul's Gospel revealed the wrath of God and the righteousness of God. It was furthermore the power of God. It was the only acceptable Gospel of Christianity. "Though we, or an angel from heaven, preach any other gospel unto you . . . let him be accursed" (Gal. 1:8). Men cannot live like Christ until they have been changed into new creatures by an experience

with Jesus. "And such were some of you: but ye are washed, but ye are sanctified, but ye are justified in the name of the Lord Jesus" (I Cor. 6:11). Paul used these words to show how some pagans had been saved by the Gospel from the abominable sins practiced in Corinth. Syncretism would ignore the very heart of the Gospel of Christ. Men are not redeemed by writing new formulas into their creeds. They do not receive the righteousness of Christ by adding new images and shrines to their collection of gods, nor by placing new names in their religious formulas. Men must experience an inward change. They must know Jesus.

What Evangelism Is

1. *The Biblical definition.* A definition of the word "evangelism" may be arrived at from a study of five Greek words found in the New Testament.

(1)   The word *euaggelidzo* in the Greek means, "I preach glad tidings." It is our word for "gospel." The verb form of the word means "to gospelize." It is often used in the New Testament and is equivalent to the word "propaganda." Jesus used it when He said, "Repent ye, and believe the gospel" (Mark 1:15). Here it means "glad tidings." The word "evangelist" is derived from this word. When Philip was designated "evangelist," the word *euaggleistas* was used (Acts 21:8). An evangelist in the New Testament sense was one who spread the good news of the kingdom.

(2)   The word *karuso* was used in connection with John, Jesus, and the early evangelists. "Jesus went about all Galilee, teaching in their synagogues, and preaching the gospel" (Matt. 4:23). Here *karuson* is used. It means "to herald." It is a picture of a messenger of an ancient king going from village to village making known a decree of the king. It is the straightforward setting forth of a truth. John came *preaching* (Matt. 3:1). He heralded the approach of a new day. To preach is to proclaim. When one preaches, he gives out a proclamation.

(3)   *Didasko* is used more often than any other word in describing the evangelism of Jesus. "Jesus went about all the cities and villages, *teaching* in their synagogues" (Matt. 9:35, italics added). He explained and unraveled the great spiritual truths in conversational fashion. He not only announced the truths, but He clarified and illustrated them. He was the master

teacher. The best evangelists will follow His example and teach and indoctrinate.

(4) The fourth word which must be considered is the word *martus*, "witness." "Ye shall be witnesses unto me" (Acts 1:8). A witness in the strict sense is a proof, an evidence. Jesus said in effect, "Ye are my proofs that Christianity is real. You are living credentials." From this word "witness" we get our word "martyr." A martyr is one who backs up his testimony with his blood. A genuine New Testament witness will preach the Gospel and will die for it also. He not only is willing to die for the Gospel but he will die to all other claims. He is set aside to one task. He is dedicated to one aim. That aim is to witness for Christ at all hazards. He may work in a factory for a livelihood, but he never loses his purpose in life. He is always a witness, a proof, a credential.

(5) The last word which elucidates the biblical definition of evangelism is *mathatas*, "disciple." "Go ye therefore, and teach [disciple] all nations" (Matt. 28:19). The Greek word is not correctly translated by "teach." *Mathateusate* is the verb form used here. It is the word "disciple." It includes more than the word "teach." It carries the idea of converting. It means more than leading a man to become a Christian. It means to instruct him also. It means to make of him a learner, a student. It means to fulfill all that is embraced in discipling.

All these words could be condensed into one word. The word is "propaganda." The early disciples did not coin the word "evangelism."[5] Evangelism was in use centuries before the Early Church was founded. "Evangelism" and "propaganda" originally meant the same thing. In the days of the disciples, "propaganda" meant something good, publicized with great effort and mighty conviction.[6] Today, the word "propaganda" has fallen into disrepute. At present, it often means the propagation of a lie under the guise of truth. But "propaganda" has a favorable connotation when used in its correct light. The evangelism of the New Testament was marked by firm conviction. When the apostles met opposition, hardships, and imprisonment, they were not moved because they were dedicated propagandists.[7]

The leaders of communism have seized upon the word "propaganda" and are seeking to thoroughly sew the world down with their ideas about economics and government. They are using every possible means to make converts. They do not hesitate to use platform, press, and every available organization to tell the world what they believe. Their system is false; their technique is clever. They offer so little, and they even use the dark passion of hate to further their ends. In spite of this, they have won much ground because they are convinced propagandists.

Christianity has so much to offer the world. It, unlike communism, offers love instead of hate, unity instead of strife, and a secure economy rather than a passing experiment. Christians should be determined propagandists. John Bunyan was thrown into prison at Bedford, England, because he refused to cease preaching. He did not stop preaching in prison. The crowds gathered outside his prison window to hear him. The authorities built high walls around the prison to keep him from preaching through the bars to the people. He raised his voice and preached out the window and over the walls to the crowds. He was an ardent propagandist.

People stoned Paul at Lystra. They stoned him because he was voicing a strange truth to them. They thought they had killed him. They left him alone with a few friends in a barren place outside their city. When Paul regained consciousness, he summoned all the physical strength which he had left and went back to Lystra. Paul was on his way to Derbe the very next day, with hollow eyes, bruised face, blood on his beard, and the love of God in his heart. Then the account says, "And when they had preached the gospel to that city, and had taught many, they returned again to Lystra" (Acts 14:21). He was a resolute propagandist. To fail to evangelize is an indictment against our modern willingness to surrender at the first signs of indifference.

2. *The definition.*

From the words which we have discussed above, we conclude that evangelism is to bear witness to the Gospel with soul aflame, and to teach and preach with the express purpose of making disciples of those who hear.

3. *The definition explained.*

(1) To bear witness with soul aflame. The inner drive which we call passion is basic in evangelism.[8] It shows itself in a burning concern which burns in the heart of the Christian as it seeks to consume all dross and every impurity. It burns until

every other ambition gives way and the one predominant desire is to bring men to know Christ as Saviour. When one is thus impelled, he goes out to labor not as a servant, but as a son. There is no clear definition of evangelism apart from this passion. It has been described as "love on fire."[9] Paul said that the love of Christ constrained him. His love for Christ became an inner urge which sent him out to witness to men. Nothing grips a man like love. One will endure hardships, cross oceans, suffer intimidations and even death, for love. It was love for lost humanity that brought Christ down from heaven to a world of sorrow to give Himself a ransom for many. This same love moved Paul to face a frowning religious and social system to preach Christ to men who had lost their way.

Jesus saw men as sheep without a shepherd and was moved with compassion (Matt. 9:36). He was not merely touched; He was moved. If He had not been moved, He never would have moved them. The evangelist must personally be moved before he can move others. This passion is not mere emotionalism. There is a difference between the deep current and the foam on the surface of the wave. The keen observer can detect the difference between the mighty currents of passion for souls and foamy emotions. When the waves come in, there will always be some foam. Don't fear the foam if it is natural. Some emotion may be expected. We should wisely guard against the excesses. But let us not forget that spiritual lethargy and moral indifference are to be feared far more than emotion. Our danger today doesn't lie in the direction of uncontrolled emotionalism; it is in the realm of a cold, passionless Christianity.

Dr. Charles Goodell calls this burning passion for souls the "inflammatory touch."[10] Dr. L. R. Elliott, one of the wisest men of our generation, warned us recently that in every age there have been those who have tried to rob evangelism of its inflammatory touch.[11] There will be influences and voices in our day which will attempt the same. But the God-conscience will die out within us before this can happen.

It is possible to talk, teach, and preach about God and have no real God-conscience. If the fires and passion of evangelism die in the preacher, they will very likely burn out in the church. A church will not soon lose its passion for souls if its preacher retains his. When the fire burns white-hot in the pastor, it will

soon blaze in the congregation. When the heart burns, the
tongue will be loosened. Dr. L. R. Scarborough used to say,
"Take your Bible and stay hot on the trail of lost souls." A
burning heart is essential in evangelism.

Only the vigorous will impress the world. In the Great
Awakening there were several schools of theology. There were
the old Calvinists, the strict Calvinists, and the Liberals. The
old Calvinists tried to get along with all factions and set up a
middle-of-the-road system which would offend none. They suc-
ceeded in avoiding the brunt of theological criticism but they
were ignored; and having no conviction, they did not attract
the masses. They soon all but disappeared. The strict Calvinists,
like Jonathan Edwards, Gilbert Tennent, and Whitefield, were
discussed, criticized, and hated by many; but they won great
hearing, converted thousands, and their group grew. Edwards
kept a close watch on excesses and guarded his group against
most of them. The Liberals grew also in spite of their innovations
and excesses. The vigorous groups always grow.

Peter burned with this passion on the day of Pentecost. A
revival broke into flame at Pentecost that lasted for four hundred
years. Chrysostom and his compatriots in the fourth century
moved on the ebbing tides of this revival.

Paul had this passion which burned in his Master's heart
when he declared, "Woe is unto me, if I preach not the gospel."
He was not fearful of physical judgment.[12] A consuming fire
burned in Paul's soul. He had to preach. If they arrested him, he
would preach to the soldiers to whom he was chained. Preaching
was not optional with him; he had to do it. Wherever he was,
there he preached. He told Timothy to preach in season and out
of season. He was saying to the young preacher, "Preach on all
occasions and do not let anyone curb you."

How shall we preserve this vital flame? We shall suggest
five ways:

(a) Cultivate it. The first impression which a new convert
has is to tell someone else about his wonderful experience with
God. If this urge is suppressed or neglected, it may die. The
passion for souls is originally there, but it may not remain
unless cultivated.

(b) Keep active in evangelism. Idleness is death.

(c) Study the Bible and the techniques of evangelism.

Often lack of knowledge is the underlying cause for the loss of this "inflammatory fire."

(d) Keep sin out of the life. Sin will quench the flame of evangelistic desire.

(e) A healthy prayer life is vital.

(2) The proclamation. Since evangelism includes a confrontation, there can be no adequate definition of evangelism apart from the Evangel, the directions given the sinner when he is confronted with Christ.

(a) The contents of the proclamation. Every message given in the New Testament magnifies Christ. The New Testament preachers told who Christ was and what they knew of Him from prophecy and experience. When Peter and John healed the lame man in the name of Jesus Christ before a large crowd at the door of the temple (Acts 3), they took no personal credit but seized upon the opportunity to tell the story of the life, death, and resurrection of Jesus. Peter concluded the witness with an appeal to the crowd to repent and believe (Acts 3:19).

At Pentecost Peter based the outpouring of the Spirit on the prophecy of Joel (Acts 2:16). He told them who Jesus was and about His great works in the earth (Acts 2:22). He spoke of His crucifixion and resurrection. He corroborated his words on the resurrection by referring to what David had said centuries before about the resurrection of the Messiah (Acts 2:25-31, Psalm 16:10). He pointed out how the resurrection proved that Christ was Lord (Acts 2:32-36). He closed with a call to faith and repentance (Acts 2:38). With slight variations, Stephen and Paul preached in the same manner. They all told the simple story of Jesus.

The Evangel contains instructions also for the sinner as to his guilty condition before God. The sinner must realize he is lost before he can be saved. As he is told the story of Jesus, God's Son, he will begin to feel that his relation to God is not right, but he is not likely to bring himself to a conviction that he is lost. "Lost" is a dark, shocking word to him, and he cringes in its presence. The task of evangelism is to help the sinner to realize his lost-ness, to stop denying it, and to turn to God for a way out. When he sees his condition before God, he will then be eager to listen to the "good news" that there is pardon for him; that God has provided a remedy. Christ is the remedy.

At this point the evangelist will inform the convicted sinner that he may receive the benefits of the remedy by faith and repentance. The simple plan of salvation will now be explained to him.

This is not intended to be an exhaustive treatment of the contents of the Gospel, but merely an abridged statement of the *kerygma* of the apostles. The Evangel of the apostles dealt with events localized in time and space, and not with abstractions. They did not concern themselves with moral homilies. They spoke of plain, hard facts. They told how God came down into history and why He came. They appealed to men to repent in the face of these revelatory truths. They urged all to believe in Christ.

(b)   The purpose of the proclamation. The apostles testified only to convince. They were not actors. It never occurred to them that they were to please their audiences. They had no idea of entertaining anyone. They preached to convince. From the opening sentence to the closing appeal, their one aim was to help men understand, perceive the truth, and change their minds about religion. They worked for a verdict. They pulled for a decision.

Those early followers of Christ were witnesses. They were determined to disciple all men. Jesus had told them, "Go ye therefore, and teach [disciple] all nations" (Matt. 28:19). Their aim was to be and make witnesses. They received the idea from Jesus. If Jesus had been preaching to please, He never would have said, "Woe unto you, scribes and Pharisees, hypocrites!" (Matt. 23:13). He had come to change the world and not merely to get along with it. At Lystra, Paul was preaching to make disciples and not to please. Nothing would have pleased that crowd of pagans at Lystra more than to have been beguiled into thinking Paul was Mercurius and Barnabas was Jupiter. They wanted to believe that Paul and Barnabas were gods from heaven honoring them with a visit. Paul and Barnabas could have received the praise and honor of gods. Instead they said, "We . . . preach unto you that ye should turn from these vanities unto the living God" (Acts 14:15). Paul refused the crown of a god and chose instead an assault with stones. He knew and declined to compromise the purpose of the *kerygma*.

(3)   The spirit of evangelism. It would be difficult to

conceive of a definition of evangelism without considering the spirit of evangelism. The spirit cannot be written into a definition, but it permeates and overshadows it. We have spoken of the Evangel, but the spirit must match the message.

(a) Courage is one of the fitting words used to describe the spirit of evangelism. The true evangelist must never give in to discouragement. He must maintain a spirit of optimism.[13] Evangelism is no task for a pessimist. The winner of souls must be an incurable optimist. Jesus was optimistic because of His faith in what He was doing. He spoke of the possibility of a little leaven leavening the whole (Matt. 13:33). He had faith that His cause would grow and gain momentum in the earth (Matt. 13:31, 32). He believed in the ultimate triumph of His cause.

Jesus was surrounded by religious prejudice, deep-rooted, racial hatred, and diverse customs long established by false thinking and practice of centuries. Greek transcendentalism and other shades of bewildering philosophies occupied the minds of men. He began His movement in a world whose political leaders were power-mad Roman dictators with pagan background. Yet His faith was stronger than all the walls and chains of circumscription which would endeavor to curb His efforts. The indomitable spirit of optimism characterized the evangelism of Christ.

His spirit of optimism was contagious. His disciples followed in His train. John, exiled on the lonely island of Patmos, continued to see Christ as a mighty conquerer (Rev. 1:13-18). He was cut off from his friends and isolated from the world, but all this could not rob him of his courage. The evangelism of John, like that of his Master, was permeated by a conquering spirit.

Paul had the same spirit which possessed Jesus and John when he said, "I can do all things through Christ which strengtheneth me" (Phil. 4:13). This was not empty boasting nor blind optimism, but rather a spirit engendered by living faith in the risen Christ. Paul did not write these words in the beginning of his ministry before he had encountered the cold, stubborn, pagan world. He had preached in Damascus and Jerusalem. He had faced determined religious leaders who were full of error. He had been stoned almost to death by the same fickle crowd which had tried to make a god of him a few hours earlier. He had come to grips with the tough Judaizers. He had done combat with almost every foe of the Christian religion. After all this and more he could say, "I can do all things through Christ." This is the testimony, therefore, not of a novice but of a seasoned veteran of the way. Experience is the greatest proof of reality.

One great realization kept courage alive in these early followers of Christ. It was the conviction that all men can and should be made disciples of Christ. Our supreme task is to lead men to accept Christ as Saviour and follow Him as Lord. "Men are not to be made champions of a Cause, or protagonists of a Doctrine, or Saviours of Society, or builders of a Church, or prophets of a Millennium, or snatchers of brands from the burning, or teachers of a philosophy of life, or proclaimers of ethical standards, or any such thing, *primarily*. Those who are in ignorance and unbelief concerning Christ, whatever their status, can and must be made *disciples (learners)* of Him who is the Way, the Truth, the Life; else the individual and society are without hope."[14]

(b) One important underlying principle deep-seated in the spirit of evangelism is sacrifice. The spirit of sacrifice cannot be artificially manufactured. It must grow naturally out of contact with Jesus and a vision of human need. Some argue that it must come solely from an experience with Jesus. Neither the New Testament nor Christian experience corroborate this view. It may sound nobler to declare that one preaches to the lost world not because of its needs but because of a love for Christ and His Gospel. Human need, however, seems to play a prominent role with the Christian and his spirit of sacrifice.

When the twelve returned from the first great evangelistic mission, Jesus took them to a secluded spot for rest and instructions. Jesus and His disciples were weary. As they were about to relax, a huge crowd which had heard of their whereabouts thronged them and broke up the retreat. Was Jesus impatient because their much needed rest had been interrupted? No, He had compassion on the crowd because of their lost-ness and began to teach them (Mark 6:34). What moved Jesus to minister to them? Was it His love for the truth only? It was their condition also, for the Word says, "They were as sheep not having a shepherd." Jesus was teaching His disciples by example one of the underlying motives of evangelism. He was teaching His disciples that one must be willing to sacrifice himself for the salvation of sinners. This spirit is as necessary as the spirit of optimism and courage. One who does not possess this spirit cannot be a winner of souls.

Jesus gave up His place at the Father's throne temporarily to live in a land of tears, graves, hatred, persecution, prejudice, and death in order to reveal to mortal men a better way. He said to His disciples, "As my Father hath sent me, even so send I you" (John 20:21). He also taught, "If any man will come after me, let him deny himself, and take up his cross daily, and follow me" (Luke 9:23).

The Christian who gives up the world and dedicates himself to discipling men will suffer many scars and know sacrifice as did his Master, but he will impress his world indelibly for good. There is no real power nor joy in the Christian life which knows nothing of sacrifice. It is the heart of the Christian way. It has never been easy in any age and never will be. Indulgence and softness are mortal enemies of Christian effectiveness. "Woe unto them that are at ease in Zion."

(c) The spirit of evangelism which is basic in soul-winning cannot endure apart from the presence and power of the Holy Spirit. The Holy Spirit empowers, illumines, preserves, and guides the soul-winner. The Holy Spirit makes Christ real to the Christian. The evangelism of the apostles became most effective after the inauguration of the Spirit on the day of Pentecost. There would be no conviction for sin, no enabling power, no mighty drive, no revolutionary proportions, without the Holy Spirit. The enthusiasm of zealous disciples would not long survive this world of sin without the burning presence of the Holy Spirit. We shall subsequently study His place in evangelism.

CHAPTER 3

DYNAMICS OF EVANGELISM

The source of evangelistic power is the Holy Spirit. Any treatise on basic evangelism must deal with the work and place of the third person of the Trinity. The great truths of the Gospel are ineffective without the power of the Holy Spirit. Power is witnessed when truth is rendered operative. "By grace are ye saved through faith" is a cardinal truth, but men become recipients of grace through the work of the Holy Spirit. There can be no world evangelization apart from the Holy Spirit. This great truth is sensed in the Lord's instructions to His disciples just before He ascended into glory when He said, "Tarry ye in the city of Jerusalem, until ye be endued with power from on high" (Luke 24:49).

The disciples were enthusiastic. They had been thoroughly taught and imbued with the truth and a vision of world need. They had witnessed the miracles Jesus worked in His great ministry. They had seen Him in His resurrected body and would soon behold the ascension. They were fired with great truth and zeal, but Jesus knew that was not enough. Jesus knew that the cold, hard world would soon sap their enthusiasm. They would meet with determined opposition, bitter criticism, and Satan stubbornly entrenched in human society. They would need more than knowledge, vision, and enthusiasm. They must have the power of God. Jesus linked His program of evangelization with the power of the Holy Spirit[1] (Acts 1:8). Jesus gave in one breath the scope, nature, and equipment of His evangelistic program. The scope was the world, the nature was witnessing, and the equipment was the enabling power of the Holy Spirit.[2]

The Holy Spirit had such a prominent part in the evangelism of the Early Church that the Book of Acts may well be titled, "Acts of the Holy Spirit." The Holy Spirit fell on its members

40

on the day of Pentecost and occasioned a revival more intensive
and longer lived than any in history. The Holy Spirit led them
step by step in an ever increasing advance in world conquest.
He led Philip to go to Samaria to conduct a revival among the
mixed breeds, possibly the first step toward world-wide evangelism (Acts 8). The Holy Spirit came upon the Gentiles as Peter
preached in the house of Cornelius, thus taking the church one
step further in global evangelism. The Holy Spirit called Paul
and Barnabas, the two first commissioned missionaries, and led
the church at Antioch to send them forth (Acts 13). He ac-
companied them to guide and empower. All the way through
the Book of Acts the followers of Christ are aware of the
presence of the Spirit. The burning presence of the Spirit is the
most noticeable phenomenon in the divine account.

To get the full significance of the work of the Holy Spirit
in evangelism, it is well to study Him in His relation to Christ,
the world, the individual Christian, and the church.

The relation of the Holy Spirit to Christ is twofold.

1.   He reveals the redemptive personality of Christ to men.

(1)   He reveals the Christ of experience. Men need a
Christ-filled dynamic.[3] Lofty ideals cannot be realized apart from
inner dynamics. Men cannot lift themselves by their own boot-
straps, however convinced and determined they may be. One's
own energy applied is insufficient. The needed power is supplied
in the redemptive work of Christ. "The gospel of Christ . . . is
the power of God unto salvation" (Rom. 1:16). How can the
soul form living contact with Christ and His meritorious work?
The answer to this question reveals the work of the Holy Spirit
in evangelism. Men are led of the Holy Spirit to have an
experience with Christ by faith. Christ is revealed by the Holy
Spirit as the answer to our moral and spiritual need. The Spirit
further shows how to receive this answer. The reception of
Christ as Saviour releases the dynamics necessary for spiritual
life.

Experience with Christ becomes the *sphere* and not the
source of our saving knowledge.[4] Some offer experience as a
proof of the reality of Christ and of eternal life. This is not the
whole truth. We live by faith, and not by experience. Experience
is the result of faith. Faith produces experience and not experience faith. The deepest in human experience does not come

from within man but from God. The grace applied by the Holy Spirit gives rise to an experience which is evidence of salvation; thus experience is the sphere and not the source of the knowledge of salvation. Men know they are saved not because they feel it, but because of the authority of God's Word; not because they feel it, but because they know Him. They come to know Him when truth is presented by a witness and empowered by the Holy Spirit. Revealed truth is without effect apart from the Holy Spirit.

(2) The Holy Spirit reveals the Christ of history. One may minimize the fact of Christ in history and go on the assumption that to experience Christ in salvation is enough. Personal experience, however, is not to be independent of historical fact. Grounds for an experience must be based upon a fact. Saving faith is not blind; it requires evidence. The Holy Spirit testifies to the historical facts of Christ. He empowers these facts when they are presented. "The Spirit searcheth all things, yea, the deep things of God" (I Cor. 2:10). Christ said of the work of the Holy Spirit, "He shall glorify me: for he shall receive of mine, and shall show it unto you" (John 16:14). The power of the personality of Christ is available only through the Holy Spirit. The Holy Spirit does not speak of Himself (John 16:13). He reveals Christ and glorifies Him. Christ is the subject of the Gospel. The Spirit illumines and empowers the Gospel.

(3) The Holy Spirit applies the redemptive work of Christ to the soul; thus, He has a vital relation to the work of Christ as well as to the person of Christ.

(a) That Christ died to save men is a redemptive fact, but the preacher must bear witness to this truth before the Holy Spirit can render it dynamic. The Holy Spirit does not operate apart from truth. When the Gospel is preached, the Holy Spirit empowers it. There is no redemption, however, apart from the truth.

(b) Christ was buried and raised from the dead, which is a redemptive fact, but the resurrection truth cannot produce a sense of justification without the operation of the Holy Spirit.

(c) The work of the Holy Spirit covers the whole life of the redeemed.[5] He regenerates (John 3:5), He sanctifies (Rom. 8:5), and He guides the lives of the redeemed individuals.

2. Relation of the Holy Spirit to the world (unregenerated mankind).

(1) He convicts of sin, righteousness, and judgment (John 16:8-11). How does He reprove the world? He alone does not reprove the world. If He did, He would supplant the church. Truly His work is to convict the world, but He does not work apart from the truth and testimony. Men in pagan lands are never convicted of the virgin birth of Christ, His mission on earth, His death, His resurrection, and other redemptive truths apart from some person bearing witness to these truths. When the truth is spoken, written, or lived by the witness, then the Holy Spirit empowers the truth to work conviction in lost men. The New Testament does not teach that the Holy Spirit convicts the world apart from the church and the truth.[6] Jesus plainly declared, "Whom the world cannot receive, because it seeth him not" (John 14:17). The writings of Paul corroborate this teaching when Paul says, "The natural man receiveth not the things of the Spirit of God: for they are foolishness unto him: neither can he know them, because they are spiritually discerned" (I Cor. 2:14). When Jesus gave His disciples the program of world evangelization, He said, "And that repentance and remission of sins should be preached in his name among all nations . . . but tarry ye . . . until ye be endued with power from on high" (Luke 24:47, 49). The disciples were to be the instruments, the Word the message, and the Spirit the power.[7] All the sermons in the world could never convict one sinner of his sins, but when the Holy Spirit breathes upon the truth, it convicts. The truth must be present in the form of spoken word, letter, or life. The Spirit works in conjunction with the truth.

(2) He regenerates the believer. Christ referred to regeneration as a birth of the Spirit (John 3:5). Paul referred to Christians as new creatures in Christ Jesus (II Cor. 5:17). Jesus declared, "He that heareth my word, and believeth on him that sent me, hath everlasting life" (John 5:24). Paul gave explanation of the above statement of Christ when he taught, "Not by works of righteousness which we have done, but according to his mercy he saved us, by the washing of regeneration, and renewing of the Holy Ghost" (Titus 3:5). Lost men who believe become sons of God through the power of God (John 1:12), but

the power of God is operative only through the work of the Spirit.

3. The relation of the Holy Spirit to the individual Christian.

The relation of the Holy Spirit begins with the individual while he is a lost sinner. When the Spirit applies the redemptive work of Christ, the sinner becomes a child of God. The Spirit then has a twofold relation to the individual: He guides the believer and He empowers him for service.

(1) He guides the believer in two realms.

(a) He guides the believer in his own relation to God. He gives the believer the knowledge of his sonship (Rom. 8:16). The Spirit bears witness with the spirit of the believer that he is one born into God's family. The Spirit also reveals to the child of God that he is an heir of God and joint-heir with Christ. The Spirit assures him of his salvation and makes known also the riches of his possession (Rom. 8:17).

(b) The Spirit guides the believer in the realm of truth. "The Spirit searcheth all things, yea, the deep things of God" (I Cor. 2:10). He is the interpreter of the Word of God. He is our best commentary. He is our most reliable authority on biblical content and meaning. He is our eyes with which to see truth. Jesus said of Him, "When he, the Spirit of truth, is come, he will guide you into all truth" (John 16:13).

(2) He indwells the believer.

(a) He indwells the believer to possess him (I Cor. 3:16). The Spirit dwells within the believer as if the believer were a temple. When one is redeemed, the Spirit comes in to live. The Spirit is a person and cannot enter partially. He is either all the way inside the temple or He is not in at all. "If any man have not the Spirit of Christ, he is none of his" (Rom. 8:9). The indwelling Spirit is an imperative. The Spirit may indwell one and not completely possess him. The tragedy is that too often Christians curb the freedom of the Holy Spirit within them by plain selfishness or ignorance, and sometimes both. They either crowd the Spirit off into a side room by worldly living, or they are wholly ignorant of His place in their lives. Though He indwells, He may not have access to the whole life. At Corinth carnality had prevented spiritual growth, and their works were cf small avail. Paul intimated that they were unaware of the indwelling Spirit. He asked, "Know ye not that ye are the temple of God, and that the Spirit of God dwelleth in you?" (I Cor. 3:16).

The individual Christian is an effective witness in world evangelization only insofar as he is possessed by the Spirit. He becomes a part of the body of Christ through the operation of the Spirit (I Cor. 12:13), but he must accept Christ as Lord of his life before he can be effective as an evangelist. When Christ is supreme in his life, the Spirit of Christ will completely possess the believer. When he is ruled by the Spirit of Christ he will think, act, live, and serve as does his Master. Paul said, "No man can say that Jesus is the Lord, but by the Holy Ghost" (I Cor. 12:3).

(b) The Spirit indwells the Christian to make intercession (Rom. 8:26). Even after a man becomes a child of God, he will still have weaknesses and often be infirm. Paul declared to the Romans that the Spirit indwelled them to help their infirmities. "Likewise the Spirit also helpeth our infirmities" (Rom. 8:26). Their greatest infirmity was prayerlessness.[8] "For we know not what we should pray for." The Spirit helps us pray as we should to get results. The intercession which He makes for us is not in heaven before the throne of God, but it is in our hearts.[9] His intercession is in conjunction with our longings and desires. Often a Christian may have a yearning or need for which he can find no conveyance in words of man. Such unspoken desires are created by the indwelling Spirit and are expressed by Him with "groanings which cannot be uttered." He helps the Christian pray. Through the centuries it has been found that Christians are effective witnesses only when they pray. No Christian has at any time been spiritually powerful who did not pray much. Prayer is a privilege and a duty. This privilege will not be claimed nor this duty performed apart from the help of the Spirit. Effective witnessing is evidence of powerful praying, and effectual, fervent praying is a sign of the indwelling Spirit. Powerlessness and prayerlessness go hand in hand with spirit-lessness. Evangelism, therefore, is utterly dependent on the dynamics of the Spirit. This leads us to the third emphasis in the relation of the Spirit to the individual.

(3) He empowers the individual for service (Acts 1:8).

Certain metaphors and symbols are used in the Bible to set

forth the presence and work of the Holy Spirit. These symbols are fire, wind, and water.

(a) "And there appeared unto them cloven tongues like as of fire" (Acts 2:3). The power of fire is understood best by those who have had special experience with it. One cannot read about the fire which all but destroyed Chicago without seeing the confusion of panicking thousands and the helplessness of men to cope with it. One cannot face the leaping tongues of fire as they sweep through a great forest without admitting its strange power. Fire is one of the most dreaded physical powers known to man.

(b) Another symbol used in connection with the Spirit is wind. Jesus said, "The wind . . . so is every one that is born of the Spirit" (John 3:8). "Wind" here is used to declare the mystery of the spiritual birth, but it also depicts the power of the Spirit. Few things could be more powerful than a hurricane or a tornado.

(c) Water is a symbol of the Spirit. Power from water has been used to turn the wheels of industry. Destructive power is often seen in mighty floods which have swept away cities and farming areas. If all the power from all the winds that ever blew could be gathered, and all the power from all the fires that ever burned could be harnessed, and all the power from all the floods that ever swirled across the land could be combined into one mighty body of power, it could not be compared to the power of the Holy Spirit in the life of one surrendered soul. When a Christian stands to witness for God he has at his disposal this power. Anyone who would dare to witness without it is either ignorant of his heritage or is hardly worthy of the name "Christian." Such power must be present because the soul-winner is in direct conflict with Satan. Dr. B. H. Carroll said, "Over the soul of that man whom you wish to lead to Christ there is an adversary whose intelligence so far surpasses yours that it cannot be mentioned in comparison, whose power transcends yours so far that they ought never to be placed side by side, who has the experience of six thousand years of conflict, who has been in direct and personal conflict with God himself, who has placed his foot upon the heart of ten thousand foes, who has brought to nought the physical strength of Samson, the intellectual culture of Solomon, the piety of David and millions more men and women — the devil!"

Jesus commissioned His disciples to evangelize the world on the basis of His power and authority. "All power is given unto me in heaven and in earth. Go ye therefore, and teach . . . and lo, I am with you alway" (Matt. 28:18-20). If you write a letter to a loved one in a distant city, place the message in an envelope, seal it, put a stamp on it, and drop it into a mailbox, the power and authority of the United States Government backs up the delivery of that message. Back of the message of the Gospel stands all the authority of God's divine government. The witness is the carrier, but he isn't unaided. He goes clothed in the power and authority of God.

4. The relation of the Holy Spirit to the church.

Since every Christian church is a communion of believers in Christ and since we understand the vital relation of the Spirit to the individual, it will be easy to grasp His relation to His church. This particular study calls, however, for careful attention. The relation of the Spirit to Christ's church is as direct as it is to the individual. When we speak of the relation of the Spirit to the church in this chapter, we refer to the local church but not to any denomination nor to the term "Church" which is generally understood as the invisible Church or the entire body of believers made up of all churches everywhere.

(1) The Spirit abides in the true church. Paul said, "By one Spirit are we all baptized into one body" (I Cor. 12:13). Since the Spirit regenerates the individual and gives him entry into the family of God, it is natural to think He unites him to Christ and makes him a member of the body of Christ.[10] The body of Christ includes all believers of all ages and all nationalities. Anyone who has been regenerated may become a member of the local church. In the Ephesian epistle, Paul spoke of a "mystery" which had been revealed to him (Eph. 3:3). He said that by revelation God had made it known to him (Eph. 3:4). This particular mystery was that Jews and Gentiles would be made part of the same body in Christ (Eph. 3:6). No longer would God use a particular nation as the agent of evangelization, but the body of believers which is made up of the redeemed from all nations has become the agent of spiritual conquest.

Christ is the head of this spiritual body (Eph. 4:15). When

Paul taught the sacred relationship of husband and wife, he likened it unto the relation of Christ to the redeemed (Eph. 5:23). As a wife is subject to her husband, so are the redeemed subject to Christ. The local believing church, therefore, is a part of this body and not merely a separate collection of redeemed individuals.[11] It is a living organism. It receives its life from Christ. He is its head. Without Christ, a local church is a spiritually dead organization. Just as life centers in the head, so do all direction and activity. Messages are sent out from the brain to all parts of the body to co-ordinate its activity. Apart from Christ any so-called church may know motion, but it will move in circles rather than follow a charted course. Just as the human body is a wonderful piece of creation, so is the consecrated church constituted more wonderful and amazing by the Spirit.

The church constitutes the body of Christ, and each individual Christian is a member of that body. As the hand, eye, ear, mouth, etc. are each a member of the human body and all together make up the body, so each redeemed member in a church has his peculiar function to perform. When all are healthy and function correctly, the result is growth. Every Christian in a given church needs all the other members, and they in turn need him. There are no unimportant members in a church. All are essential to the life and progress of the church. Each has a task to perform. If one falls short, all suffer. The only way that Christianity today can retain the vigor of the Christianity of the New Testament era is for all redeemed to be active as members of the body of Christ. Every Christian has a personal and individual experience with God in salvation, but he must then identify himself with the local segment of the body of Christ.

(2)   The Holy Spirit provides the atmosphere for all Christian church activity.

(a)   Worship must be "in spirit" (John 4:24). One cannot worship God apart from the Spirit. Paul said, "For we are the circumcision, which worship God in the spirit" (Phil. 3:3). Many believe that the main business of the church is to develop and keep unbroken the correct relationship to Christ as Saviour and Lord.[12] This can be done by worship, and therefore worship is the most important business of the church.[13] The forms of worship vary, but that is not as important as is the dependence on the Spirit in worship. Dr. Conner never thought more clearly than when he pressed home the idea that Spirit-filled worship is most important in the life of a church. Evangelism is utterly dependent upon it. It is those who come to worship who go out to evangelize. Unfortunately all who come to worship do not evangelize, but it is from the group which worships that our soul-winners come.

(b) Witnessing is done in the power of the Spirit (Acts 2:4). The church becomes a connecting agent through the Spirit. The Spirit builds the church by adding such as are saved from day to day.

(c) Fellowship is in the Spirit (Phil. 2:1). The true church is a fellowship of the redeemed. They have much in common. They have had alike a transforming experience with God. They have similar joys, responsibilities, and problems. There is encouragement and great strength in fellowship of kindred spirits. They come together to share their experiences, to tell of victories as well as defeats. "And being let go, they went to their own company, and reported all that the chief priests and elders had said unto them. And when they heard that, they lifted up their voice to God with one accord. . . . And when they had prayed, the place was shaken where they were assembled together; and they were all filled with the Holy Ghost, and they spake the word of God with boldness" (Acts 4:23-24, 31). It is seen from this Scripture that in hours of trial the early disciples received great boldness by fellowship. The truly Christian church from the beginning has been composed of a free and voluntary group of saved people. It is a congregation of people with similar experiences and beliefs. They hold a common faith. They could have remained aloof but necessity, love, and the Holy Spirit drew them together. Just as a magnet draws steel, so the Christian church draws redeemed souls with a hunger for fellowship in Christ. The church is a family held together by the cords of love and faith. Just as there must be a seat of authority in the home, must there be authority in the church, but this authority is subject to fellowship and not fellowship subject to authority.

CHAPTER 4

THE EVANGELISTIC CHURCH

THE ORIGIN OF THE CHURCH

Jesus had but one mission on this earth, and that mission was to seek and to save the lost. When Jesus called Zacchaeus out of the sycamore tree, went home with him for lunch, and won him to salvation in the face of the criticism of the people who witnessed it, He justified His actions by saying, "the Son of man is come to seek and to save that which was lost." Jesus said unto His disciples, "As my Father hath sent me, even so send I you." It was the purpose of Christ to use His disciples to win the world to Himself. Thus, Jesus instituted the church for this definite purpose. He intends that His church shall perform many other tasks, but its supreme task is to bring the lost to Christ.

THE DEFINITION OF THE CHURCH

Is the Christian church still a vital, regenerating factor in a decadent world? Or, has it been supplanted by eleemosynary institutions and other organizations? Many of us believe that it has not been supplanted; that no organization can take its place; that it not only seeks to win the lost, but also provides a wholesome atmosphere in which civilized governments, educational institutions, and other institutions for the welfare of man may well exist. It is impossible to contain the definition of an evangelistic church in a formulary statement. A church which from pulpit to primary department works passionately to see people continually coming to Christ is evangelistic. Many of our churches, large and small, rural, village, town, and city, do have pastors, church officers, and Sunday School teachers permeated with the desire to see people find Christ as Saviour. They are trying to bring all possible to this necessary experience. However, some of our churches are not this evangelistic. Every

50

church should be evangelistic. Every member must become a soul-winner. The program of evangelism of the New Testament is dedicated to this aim.

The local Christian church could possibly be defined as a body of believers in Christ banded together by covenant for worship, Bible study, prayer, fellowship, service, and world evangelization. The church impregnable and invincible, marching in constant and undeniable triumph, is the church evangelizing.[1] When one reads the New Testament in search of a definition of the church, he does not find two distinct terms: one, a church; and the other, an evangelistic church. They are both one and the same on the pages of the New Testament. The truth is the church is not defined per se in the New Testament, but the New Testament definition follows from a description of the nature and work of the church. The work of evangelism is primarily the task of the church. Unattached and unauthorized evangelism is generally short lived and unwise. All the work of the Christian faith is centered in the local church. When any phase of our Christian work is ungoverned by the church, it may do little good and great harm. Evangelism must always be vitally related to the church or it is not evangelism. Evangelism is an imperative for the local church. The church which ceases to evangelize neglects one of its primary reasons for existing and begins the process of decline. The church is dedicated to the task of training its members and leading them to worship God, but first it must have members to develop. A body of redeemed folk cannot worship unless they exist. People must first be converted before they will accept divine truth. If the converting activity ceases, so will the converting agent. The life of a church depends on evangelism.

THE NATURE OF THE CHURCH

The word "church" appears in the New Testament one hundred and fourteen times, and eighty-eight per cent of the times it refers to the local church. Much is said today about the universal church, thus using the word "church" in the collective sense, but it is well to remember that even the collective idea must find concrete, individual expression in the local church. In this particular study of the church and for the purposes of this chapter, we shall deal with the local idea altogether.

1. The churches of the New Testament were aggressively evangelistic.[2] They were products of an aggressive evangelism. Missionaries, with the world's need in their hearts, founded these churches and taught them. The origin and background of these churches were evangelistic. Jesus predicted the evangelistic aggressiveness of these New Testament churches when He said, "Upon this rock I will build my church; and the gates of hell shall not prevail against it" (Matt. 16:18). The word "prevail" is the key word in the interpretation of this statement of Jesus. Some think this word "prevail" indicates that the gates of hell are on the offensive and the church is on the defensive, but that the gates of hell will never completely swallow up the church. This is not what it means. The word "prevail" is a compound Greek word. The word "strength" and the word "against" make up the compound word "prevail." Therefore it means "strength against." So, to use this particular word is to place the gates of hell on the defensive and the church of the living God on the offensive, because it plainly says that the gates of hell shall not have the strength to stand up against the mighty onslaughts of the church. The picture here is of an aggressive group that cannot be curbed nor stopped by any spiritual power in the universe.

2. The history of the New Testament churches verifies the truth that they were aggressively evangelistic. The church at Antioch under the direction of Barnabas and Saul prosecuted an intensive effort to evangelize the entire area around it (Acts 11:26). They were not satisfied with winning and teaching hundreds within reach of the local church, but they laid their hands on Barnabas and Saul and sent them out to Asia Minor to evangelize in many other places (Acts 13:1-3). This evangelistic program pursued by the church at Antioch in Syria was totally free from selfishness. They gave up their two best leaders for the missionary task. They might have kept these great men, who had led them with such notable success, and have sent others; but they did not. They followed the promptings of the Holy Spirit and sent Barnabas and Saul. Many things point up the value of an evangelistic church. We shall consider some of them.

THE IMPORTANCE OF THE EVANGELISTIC CHURCH

1. Evangelism is a mandate to the local church from its Lord. "Ye shall be witnesses unto me *both in Jerusalem,* and in

all Judea, and in Samaria, and unto the uttermost part of the earth" (Acts 1:8, italics added). The church is expected by its Lord to witness in the area of its location. That is included in the primary purpose of its existence. Its most pressing obligation is the area at its door. However, if it is truly evangelistic, it will not stop there. It will remember the rest of the mandate, "both in Jerusalem, Judea, and Samaria, and unto the uttermost part."

2. The pattern is outlined in the New Testament. When the Jerusalem church was persecuted, its members were scattered over the land. As they went, they told the gospel story in every town or city to which they came. Some of them who came to Antioch and preached the Lord Jesus were from Cyprus and Cyrene. A great number believed and turned to the Lord. Here Gentiles, as well as Jews, were given the Gospel and converted. The church at Jerusalem sent a capable man, named Barnabas, to investigate and strengthen the new work. Because of his helpfulness and wise counsel, "much people was added unto the Lord" (Acts 11:24). Barnabas saw that the field was ripe and sought out Paul, a new convert, to come help him preach and teach. The two zealous and consecrated men spent an entire year leading the church at Antioch in an evangelistic and conservation program. Soon the church at Antioch, directed by the Holy Spirit, separated Paul and Barnabas unto the special work of evangelizing. Paul and Barnabas went from there to Seleucia and on to Cyprus, Perga, Antioch in Pisidia, and elsewhere. It was the policy of the New Testament churches for their members to push out into new communities and preach the Gospel, win new converts, and organize them into local churches. These in turn evangelized the community where they were located and pushed out into new areas repeating the same pattern. It was Paul's practice to go back to these young organizations, instructing them and providing them competent leadership to guide them in the program of evangelizing (Acts 14:21-28).

This was the pattern followed by John Wesley in the eighteenth century. Wesley, influenced by George Whitefield, preached his first field sermon in Briston, England, May 2, 1739.

This was also the pattern followed by the Presbyterians, Baptists, and others, in the Great Awakening as they evangelized the southern colonies.

Shubal Stearns and Daniel Marshall moved from Connecticut to Virginia in 1754 and from Virginia to Sandy Creek in North Carolina in 1755 to use the same pattern of evangelization laid out in the New Testament and followed by their Presbyterian brethren. They organized Sandy Creek Baptist Church with sixteen members. In a short time the church had done so well at its task of evangelizing that it had six hundred members. Five years later this church had "mothered" or "grandmothered" forty-two churches. From this great center of operation, Baptist preachers and workers traveled in every direction preaching in every community, winning converts, and organizing them into small churches to be instructed and directed in winning their world to Christ.[3]

History tells us how local churches continued as converting agencies. Great churches like Spurgeon's Tabernacle, the Moody Church, Henry Ward Beecher's Brooklyn Church, and Chrysostom Church at Constantinople live forever in history to remind the local church of what can be done. Great numbers of small and ordinary churches, too, have been used of God to win the thousands to Christ. The location or size of the church is not significant. Churches on foreign fields with poor equipment and small numbers are winning impressive numbers of eternal souls to God.[4] All this must impress the local church with its imperative command and its importance as God's chosen instrument for world evangelization.

3. Evangelism is essential to growth. God has no other plan for the growth of His churches and the expansion of Christianity. Long centuries before the Christian Era, God said to His people, "Enlarge the place of thy tent . . . spare not, lengthen thy cords, and strengthen thy stakes" (Isa. 54:2). Later through His Son, He said, "Go ye therefore, and disciple all nations. . . . Teaching them to observe all things" (Matt. 28:19-20).[5] Though these two statements were made at least seven hundred and fifty years apart, they are the same in essence. "Spare not, strengthen thy cords" was a command to enlarge. "Go ye therefore, and disciple all nations" defines the boundaries of the "tent." A prayerful search of the Bible and God's plan for His people will clearly reveal that evangelism is most prominent and essential in God's plan for church growth.

The church at Jerusalem was an evangelistic church. It grew rapidly. What were the reasons for the great growth? The answer is found in Luke's statement, "and the Lord added to the church daily such as should be saved" (Acts 2:47). First, it grew daily. Every day new converts were made and added to the church. Its growth was not spasmodic but by continuous daily advance. In the second place, it grew through the help of God.[6] Its growth did not come merely through human ingenuity. "The Lord added . . . those who had been saved." The church members, imbued with the Spirit of God, gave their witness and the Holy Spirit used their testimony. Growth came through a daily witness empowered by the Lord.

Any church anywhere will grow if it is evangelistic. The author knows of many churches which show substantial growth each year even though they are located in most difficult fields. It will be sufficient here to point out only one. Such a church is located in a southern city where Roman Catholics dominate the community. The pastor is a good preacher but not noted for his pulpit eloquence. The church is not wealthy and owns no impressive building. It is composed of redeemed people from ordinary life. That church has the respect of even the Catholic laymen of the city. It baptizes over three hundred per year. It is crowded with worshipers each Sunday. It is a beehive of organized evangelistic activity. In contrast, many other churches in the same city and of the same persuasion show meager results for their labors each year. This particular church and its sister churches which are all having remarkable growth are tireless in their soul-winning efforts.

All of us know churches that are strategically located but are still without visible results. The location of a church has much to do with its growth, but more important than the location are the vision and zeal of such a church. An evangelistic church is God's instrument for winning the world. Dr. L. R. Scarborough says, "The value of an evangelistic church is beyond human computation. . . . The world can never be won to Christ by revivals only."[7] This great Baptist teacher and evangelist believed that if we are to win the world it must be done by the churches, and that it is a perennial task. The purpose of the revival is to quicken the spiritual heartbeat of God's people and spur us on to win the lost. However, world evangelization is a year-in and year-out job for the local churches.

4. The importance of the evangelistic church is also seen

in the strategic position of the church in the community. The church has direct and intimate access to the home. The home is vital to the life of a nation. It is from the homes that educators, statesmen, authors, builders, criminals, and undesirables come. If the ties of home are weakened and proper training is affected, the devil stands a chance to destroy a whole people. If bright, healthy fires of spiritual life crackle in the churches, they are sure to reach and lift the character of the homes. The church can have, and should have, an intimate contact with this citadel of humanity.

The church can and should have vital contact with business since many of the great leaders in commerce are members of the churches. If soul-winning fires burn brightly in the churches, it will warm those who control the tides of commerce. It will make for fair practice and honest, healthy, business principles. No economy can long endure which is built on dishonesty and avarice. An evangelistic church cannot but make virile the economy of a community.

The church should have access to the schools of the land, both directly and indirectly. If the spirit of Christ prevails in the local church, it should be able to affect the philosophy of our schools. If our churches can move our school systems closer to the heart of God, our children will be given a Christian interpretation of life, rather than an atheistic and materialistic philosophy. The faith of our children is often undermined in schools by leaders who are not under the influence of Christianity. Evangelism is not optional with the local church. It is imperative also in the realm of education.

5. Evangelism in the local church engenders liberality. If the members of a given church can be led to love lost souls enough to give time and energy to win them locally, they can also be led to give of their income to carry the Gospel to lost men around the world. When men are motivated by love for Christ and concern for the lost, they will give their possessions as well as themselves. The well-taught and truly evangelistic church will be motivated by a consuming love for Christ. Covetousness should not live in the heart of a soul-winner. "A man cannot keep his soul hot after lost men and be covetous."[8]

The church at Antioch in Syria was so fervent in its evangelistic zeal that the followers of Christ "were called Christians first in Antioch" (Acts 11:26). The church at Antioch could not be satisfied with evangelizing only Antioch, and thus it was the first church to officially send out evangelists to new territory to preach Christ (Acts 13:3-4). This same church at Antioch so abounded with liberality that it sent financial help to the poor at Jerusalem (Acts 11:29-30), while it was evangelizing Antioch and the regions beyond.

6. Evangelism at the home base will promote an interest in missions abroad. An unprecedented upsurge in evangelism in America in the nineteen-fifties has led to unparalleled liberality for missions. The executive secretaries of the various states have supported without reserve the programs of evangelism in their states. Only the Judgment will reveal how much they have meant to evangelism in America. These men know that such an emphasis at the home base cannot but bless the cause of Christ around the globe.

One needs only to read history or to observe what takes place around him to be convinced that evangelism opens hearts and purses. To be sure we mean healthy, biblical evangelism and not the spurious kind, which is a parasite on the limbs of the church begging money for itself. Two illustrations will suffice. We have pointed out already how liberality abounded in the evangelistic churches of the New Testament. Now we would point up that this great truth is still operative. Recently, an ordinary church in a town of less than fifteen thousand was challenged by its pastor to answer the evangelistic and missionary challenge. The year before, the church baptized less than fifty. It also gave less than a hundred dollars a month to missions. The church answered the challenge and became a veritable beehive of organized evangelistic activity. Within seven years, one-fifth of the population of the town united with that church. Its auditorium was filled to overflowing Sunday after Sunday, and its gifts to missions and benevolence exceeded thirty thousand dollars annually. In fact, the church today gives as much to missions as any church in that state and more than ninety-five per cent of the sister churches. This is not a rare example, for there are hundreds of churches in the land which have experienced similar growth and blessings. God has no respect of person or church. He is waiting and eager to bless all. If a church is in financial difficulty, let it prayerfully build a fire in the evangelistic furnace. If a great denomination needs more money and more mission volunteers for foreign missions, let it look upon the fields all around it, which are white unto harvest.

Some Advantages of Local Church Evangelism

1. The local church lives permanently in the local community. It stands there to minister, day in and day out. The pastors, educational directors, and music leaders may move away and be replaced by others. Some of the members may move away and new ones come in, but the church remains.[9] The local folk know the history of the local church. They have been impressed by its Gospel and the lives of its members. The church builds trust and confidence in the community. The local church is not, therefore, a "fly-by-night" agent. If it is what it should be, it is in a better position to win the lost people around it than any other organization. Besides, almost no one else can win them for Christ if the local church fails in its ministry.

2. The local church is down at the grassroots. It is not an institution removed from the heart throbs of the people. It is there where defeats and victories, tears and joys are experienced. It is not an extraneous movement with only lofty ideals and preachments. It is the body of Christ in a given community. It is made up of local citizens who have been saved by the grace of God and who long to see their fellows come to Christ. It is a family of the children of God. The church loves and cares. Right out of the heartbeat of the local church comes the evangelistic advantage.

3. The evangelism of the local church is simple, and in its simplicity we find a decided advantage. It preaches the glorious Gospel Sunday after Sunday in its regular services. It often employs special evangelistic services. It teaches the Bible constantly, and through its burning truth many find the Lord. It serves the community through its various organizations and multi-ministries. The church is a living body, and a living body must renew its life or die. Through discipling the prospects at its door, it can renew its life and grow. Its program of evangelism is as simple as that.

The Essentials of an Evangelistic Church

1. The church must have a vision of her mission in the world. This will create a wholesome dedication to the task. After

the church has been led to see this responsibility, it will be an easy step to bring it to concern. A sympathetic and concerned church can be trained and led to evangelize. If the local church has a well-rounded conception of its missionary task, it will not overlook the welfare and spiritual life of its own members. The local members must be called to deeper spiritual life. They must be consecrated. Dr. Billy Graham says that church members must be evangelized. He declares that eighty per cent of our evangelistic opportunity in America is within the churches themselves. There will be no spiritual birth of the souls of those around us until there is travail among church members. This necessary travail grows out of concern; concern grows out of sympathy; sympathy out of vision; and vision out of a solid effort to acquaint our people with the content and impact of the Gospel. If the local church stays spiritually healthy and concerned, it will have eyes with which to see the fields white unto harvest in lands afar. It will have the whole world in its heart. It will evangelize at home and abroad at the same time. If it neglects either for long, it will eventually neglect both entirely.

2. It is essential that the church keep the "seeking note." Jesus said to His disciples, "As my Father hath sent me, even so send I you." The mission of the church is similar to the mission of Christ. Jesus came to seek and to save that which is lost. To accomplish this task, the church must do many things. It will worship. It will build schools to educate its leaders and evangelists. It will look after the needs of the suffering. But everything must be subservient to finding and winning the unsaved. It is possible for a church to become so engaged in hospitalization, education, and the like that it neglects its primary purpose and fails to seek and save the lost. I repeat, such is possible; but it should not occur. The enterprise of building a barn should not make the farmer forget why he erected the building. To build a barn and to fail to plant seeds, cultivate the soil, and gather the harvest would be nonsense. What purpose would the building serve? It becomes the duty of someone to keep properly co-ordinated all the activities of the church. This privilege belongs to the pastor. If he keeps a well-balanced perspective and persistently teaches his congregation, the church will do effectively and wisely the work assigned to it by the Master. As long as the pastor has the seeking note, so will the church.

No church will remain evangelistic without the seeking note.

The pastor must be concerned with the attitude of his laymen toward the conversion of the lost. Some pastors seem to prefer doing all the soul-winning. They tend to look askance on the laymen who would be aggressive in soul-winning. Some laymen are diffident of taking the lead. Such an attitude on the part of pastor or laymen stems strictly from ignorance of the commission of the Saviour. The pastor must create the seeking note in the laymen and help them realize that evangelism is both their obligation and privilege.

If the local church fails to have a missionary spirit, of course it will fail to do local evangelism. But if a church is possessed of a missionary spirit and prosecutes vigorously a program of evangelism, no amount of resistance will be able to discourage or curb it. The strategy of evangelism employed by the local church will depend for its success on the true evangelistic spirit of the church.

3. The correct atmosphere. The entire atmosphere of the church must be permeated with a sense of God's presence. If there is a sense of God's presence, there will also be a revival atmosphere in which the souls of men can be born again. Anyone who has had the opportunity to deal with a large number of churches in many areas will be able to recognize the evangelistic atmosphere wherever he finds it. It can never be mistaken. Dr. William E. Biederwolf defines the atmosphere as "the spiritual influence created by the thoughts and feelings and dispositions of those in attendance upon the service [of the church]."[10] I should like to add that this spiritual influence, which Dr. Biederwolf says is created by the thoughts, feelings, and dispositions of those in attendance upon the service, must be shot through with a consciousness of the presence of God. When this state exists, there will be a wholesome, contagious, evangelistic enthusiasm. If this atmosphere does not exist in the church, preaching will be generally ineffective. When this desired atmosphere does exist in a church, any preaching, so long as it is true to the Bible, will get results. Many things enter to make possible such a healthy evangelistic atmosphere. This atmosphere may be nurtured in any church. It is necessary that the whole tone of the church be guarded. It is necessary that stilted dignity be dismissed. Every church service should be directed with dignity.

When the pastor and congregation lose their poise, they have lost their opportunity and their effectiveness to capture the mind and will of the guests present. But this dignity must not be a false dignity. It must not be the cold, stilted type. If the evangelistic atmosphere is to be created and maintained, the church must be free from the frivolous. The preacher should never joke at the expense of the spirit of his service and the effectiveness of his sermon. Often, the blessing of an excellent song service, which has built a deep spirit for the sermon, has been lost by a few frivolous remarks at the introductory part of the message. This is always sad, unfortunate, and unnecessary. The tone of the service should be one of reverent gladness.[11] People can manifest a spirit of gladness pulsating with hopefulness without bordering at all on the frivolous. A bright, reverent service, filled with expectation and gladness, always makes for a wholesome atmosphere.

4. It is absolutely essential that unity prevail in the church. "And when the day of Pentecost was fully come, they were all with one accord in one place" (Acts 2:1). This passage of Scripture sets forth the unmistakable truth of the power of unity. They were one in purpose. They were one in spirit. They were in accord in their experience and beliefs. They came together with great expectation. Sermons are ineffective in an atmosphere of disunity. The Spirit of God cannot thrive in the midst of broken fellowship. The people must believe the same fundamental truths. They must love the same things of the Spirit. They must be concerned in the same way about mankind; and they must be ready to work together for the Lord. Unity is as essential to evangelism as it is to the life of the church. "If any man have not the Spirit of Christ, he is none of his" (Rom. 8:9). The same thing can be said of the church. The Spirit of Christ must prevail, and the Spirit of Christ has no part in disunity.

5. It is always essential that the members of the church be consecrated to evangelism. The New Testament church was set apart for the task of winning men to Christ. When the members of the church have been dedicated to the task of evangelism, it will be necessary to continually promote it. Dr. Sweazey reminds us that a church never grows toward evangelism; it drifts away from it.[12] Those who have had even a small amount of experience with churches will agree without argument that Dr.

Sweazey is correct. If this is true, then we realize immediately the importance of continual promotion. The tendency is to place evangelism last on the list of "musts." We visit the sick, get out the bulletin, plan our staff and group meetings, attend the associational gatherings, read current religious articles, prepare messages, and if any time is left, it may be used to contact the lost. The churches must continually be reminded and urged to evangelize. Evangelism must be promoted in the modern local church. We do only the things which we plan and promote. The church members do what they have been led to believe is important. They will never see soul-winning as a vital part of their Christian living unless the church magnifies it through every available avenue of thought communication. We must promote evangelism through bulletins, sermons, conferences, and every church organization.

Chapter 5

PASTORAL EVANGELISM

The greatest single need in evangelism today is pastoral evangelism. This statement does not imply that every-member evangelism and revival efforts are not vital. It simply means that without pastoral evangelism there will be no every-member evangelism, nor much of any other kind.

The place of the pastor in the evangelism of the local church is strategic. If he is evangelistic, the church will ordinarily be evangelistic. The degree to which the pastor is evangelistic will be reflected in the church. If he is lukewarm, the church will very likely be likewise. If he is intensely evangelistic, the church will reflect the warmth and concern of the pastor. The pastor has certain advantages that no other individual in the church, or connected with the church, has. He has a constant and intimate access to his people which gives him every advantage over any denominational leader or anyone else. This should be the case, but along with it goes the responsibility to lead the church to do the work which it is designed to do. The people have learned to love and follow the pastor because of his helpful contacts in sickness, marriage, and death. He may often preach poorly, but his people will esteem him because he is someone special to them. This, and the fact that he is constantly before them on Sundays preaching the Gospel, gives him an entree to their hearts, which is singular in human relations. This does not imply that the pastor is to do all the soul-winning, but rather that he is in a better position to lead the church to evangelize than anyone else.

There are some instances in which the pastor feels his evangelistic responsibility so keenly that he tries to do all the soul-winning. This is an error. He must set the example and then lead the entire church membership to follow.

63

A devastating heresy today is found in the belief that the pastor should do all the soul-winning while the church indulges in complacency.[1] Jesus meant it when He said, "Go ye therefore, and disciple all nations."[2] He was speaking to His church and not merely to the pastor. Often those guilty of this heresy are not aware of the seriousness of it. Just as often, they are not consciously aware of the heresy. Recently a pastor, at the end of a five-year period of his pastorate, awakened his congregation by recounting the number of additions by baptism which the church had received during this five-year period. Then he asked all to rise who could claim to have been responsible in any way at all for any of the conversions. He gave ample time for reflection, but not a person rose. The congregation was shocked. It had a telling effect on the people. Within a few weeks twenty-two were received into the membership of the church by baptism. Twenty of these had been won by members of the congregation.[3]

The vital place of the pastor in church evangelism is pointed up in a marked way by the fact that churches of all denominations cease to have any appreciable number of additions while they are without a pastor. It is practically impossible to conduct a successful revival meeting in a church while it has no regular minister. No amount of preparation, visitation, or good preaching can make up for the absence of the pastor. There are almost no exceptions to this rule. This certainly magnifies the strategic position of the pastor in leading a church in witnessing.

Many denominational leaders believe that the reason for so large a number of churches reporting from none to less than a half-dozen conversions each year in all of the major denominations is due in part to the large turnover in pastors. Also many of these churches have part-time pastors and others are without adequate oversight and direction. Every believer should be a discipler. History records that every believer is a potential discipler, but as a rule he will not witness effectively without pastoral direction and inspiration.

We shall seek to elaborate on three thoughts in this chapter. First, some characteristics of the evangelistic pastor; second, the pastoral opportunities for evangelism; and lastly, the pastor's program of evangelism.

Every pastor can be evangelistic. The temperament and nature of some pastors will make it easier for them to be evangelistic than it is for others; but all may, and should, develop the gift. Dr. A. W. Blackwood says, "If the pastor is of the reflective temperament he may confine himself to the care of the sheep and refuse to engage in anything evangelistic."[4] There are also contrasting cases where the pastor may have such a consuming desire to win the lost that he works at evangelism without any concern for his other important pastoral duties. The truth is that many pastors have excelled in performing all pastoral duties, as well as evangelism. It is not a question of either/or. The pastor's task includes both. Both can be accomplished by the diligent pastor at the same time.

Too often the young minister gets the idea that his pulpit ministry is the main thing in his life. Every pastor must study and do his best in the pulpit. However God called the minister to the pastorate. Pastoral duties are not optional. "To preach is one of the duties of the ministry, but it is only one."[5]

CHARACTERISTICS OF THE EVANGELISTIC PASTOR

1. Every pastor has certain basic beliefs. He should believe that men are lost. He should believe that unsaved men are under "the wrath of God" (John 3:36). If he does not hold this belief he will never warn men, nor will there be urgency in his message. The evangelistic pastor is aware that there is a fundamental wrongness in the hearts of men. He will earnestly seek to bring them into contact with the spiritual therapy of forgiveness. Without forgiveness of God, there can be no reconciliation.

Every minister must believe that Christ is the Saviour. If he has no conviction at this point, he may accept almost any kind of substitute for salvation. He may feel that men can save themselves. He may feel that men can be saved by works.

He must believe that he is divinely called of God. The pastoral ministry is not a profession to be chosen by man. God makes the choice. Preaching is divine. One may greatly improve his effectiveness by study and observation, but preaching is, first of all, a gift to be exercised and not just an art to be learned. Anyone who has preached often has learned that he may preach with great liberty today, but tomorrow, after the same amount of study and prayer, fail miserably. Preaching is of God. Every preacher is wholly dependent upon God.

2. The evangelistic pastor must have intellectual ability.

To lead a church into successful evangelism requires intellectual power. It is no ordinary task. Tactful diplomacy and keen perception are essential for winning men to Christ and teaching others the art of soul-winning. Creative thinking and organizational ability are also valuable assets. A telling example of this is found in the case of Richard Baxter at Kidderminster. Kidderminster was a small city of less than five thousand people, and the people were for the most part well fixed and financially secure. The former pastor, who had served before the coming of Baxter, was weak in every respect. His curate was a common drunkard. The people were in deep spiritual darkness as a result of such a lack of capable pastoral leadership. Richard Baxter employed three techniques, which proved most effective. In the first place, he was a passionate and earnest preacher of the Gospel. He preached every time "as a dying man to dying men." At first, the people did not receive him well, but soon he became very popular. His church filled to capacity, and it became necessary for them to add many balconies to care for the ever increasing congregation. In the second place, he employed a unique type of personal evangelism. He arranged for every family in his parish to come to his house, one by one. He would spend at least one hour in his home speaking with that family about spiritual matters and about soul salvation. Then he would take each member of the family apart and tenderly urge upon them to make a decision for the Lord Jesus Christ. Most of the families were won. Every family was greatly affected. The third technique employed by the brilliant and intellectual pastor was to lead the families to set up family worship in their homes. As a result, Kidderminster became a veritable colony of heaven in an hour of general spiritual darkness and wickedness.[6]

Richard Baxter was a man of great intellectual ability. He had one of the sharpest minds of his generation. He was a master of mathematics, physics, and medicine. Being a man of great ability and many talents, it was possible for him to meet the challenge in a crucial hour in the history of his nation and in the history of his local community.

If one wished to multiply illustrations, he could easily call attention to Jonathan Edwards, who had the keenest mind of his generation. He was considered one of the greatest philosophers, theologians, and teachers of his day. Mr. Edwards was also creative enough and prolific enough to be used of God to see in his own church the first signs of what came to be known as the Great Awakening.

3. The pastor is a priest and a prophet. The priest in the Old Testament was a go-between for God and man. It was his purpose to get God and man together. His office was one of reconciliation. The functions of the priests of the Old Testament are ascribed to the pastor in the New Testament. He represents men before God and God before men.[7] He represents Christ before men, and he intercedes to God for men. As priest he stands with men and pleads their cause before God. He is also a prophet. As a prophet, he stands with God and warns and instructs the people. Every pastor, by nature of his office, is priest and prophet. The office of reconciliation implies soul-winning by the very nature of its operation.

4. The evangelistic pastor must have the correct attitude. The evangelistic pastor must be genuinely sincere. David Hume once listened to John Brown of Haddington and said, "I like that man, for he preaches as if Christ were in the pulpit with him."[8] If the pastor is in dead earnest and if he actually loves lost men, it will show up in his sermons and in his conduct. For more than forty years in London, C. H. Spurgeon took time to win at least one man a day outside his pulpit ministry. D. L. Moody, the great evangelist of another generation, was one of the busiest men of his day as an evangelist, teacher, and educator; but he took time out to bow alongside of, personally deal with, and win to Christ no less than 750,000 people in his lifetime. It was said of Mr. Moody that he could hardly wait until he had finished his sermon to go to the inquiry room to talk with people individually. There was a consuming love in his heart. He had a burning interest for lost men and a great desire to see them right in the sight of God. A spirit like that of Spurgeon, Moody, Baxter, and many others who could be mentioned, is a contagion. Spirit-impelled, soul-seeking pastors will do much to lead their congregations to become soul-winners.

5. The evangelistic pastor must be a man of prayer. No man will have power with men who does not first have power with God, and no man can have the power of God within him unless he rubs shoulders often with God in the spirit of prayer. History fails yet to record one successful evangelist or evange-

listic pastor who was not a man of prayer. Every pastor must give careful consideration to his own devotional life. There must be a time set aside every day when he will, for his own good, read the Bible and pray.

John Tauler of the fourteenth century, who lived in Strasbourg, was the most powerful preacher of his generation. People came miles and miles to hear him. One day he became conscious of the fact that he was preaching more to excel than to bless the hearts of men and to glorify God. He closed the door of his office and spent long hours in prayer. When the time came for him to preach on Sunday and the crowds had gathered from all over Europe, the attendants wondered why Master Tauler had not appeared in the pulpit. When it was past time for him to preach, they went into his study and found him on his knees in prayer. They urged him to come and preach to the great waiting audience, but Tauler said to them, "Go back and tell the audience I will not preach today. Neither shall I ever preach again unless God comes with me into the pulpit." For long days Tauler prayed, and the people continued to come back to hear him. Finally, when he came to his pulpit, he came in such power that many people within a few minutes of his sermon were so convicted that they fell prostrate along the benches, in the aisles, and upon the floor. Tauler was able to use the method of prayer to bring about a great turning to God in his day. For a hundred and fifty years, Tauler and his example blessed the hearts of the people of Europe through the influence of prayer circles he set in motion.

All of these essentials so necessary to pastoral evangelism are latent within every pastor and can be developed. They may be developed by a constant study of history, becoming more and more familiar with successful evangelistic pastors and great evangelists of the past, and studying their lives and methods to catch something of their spirit. They may also be developed by keeping a close watch upon one's own devotional life and continuing to pray and study and read for one's own good. They may also be developed by going among the people and observing the way they live, the way they die, the way they rejoice, the way they grieve. When a pastor seeks to help them, there will be created within his own heart a consuming desire to win souls for Christ until the whole world comes to know God and what it means to have peace in God.

PASTORAL OPPORTUNITIES

1. Pastoral evangelism is the answer to the spiritual needs of the city. Ten years ago a small church of one hundred and thirty members in a residential area of Waco, Texas, called a pastor whose heart burned for the lost. Today a beautiful church building is filled with the most faithful and consecrated worshipers one ever saw. They gather every Sunday to praise God from whom all blessings flow. Their record sets forth the account of a small struggling church which was to be blessed with an amazing growth within one decade by proven methods of pastoral evangelism. Thousands of other churches in the land have evangelized great city areas as effectively as has the Waco church. Any church in any urban area will grow with amazing rapidity if its pastor, zealous for the Lord, employs the best methods of pastoral evangelism.

2. Pastoral evangelism is the answer to the seemingly doomed spots in the areas of the land. We mean by "doomed spots" certain areas like the downtown areas and the "static areas." The scientists say that the conditions of a thing must be right or the thing will not survive. The scientists go on to say that if you have a flower of any kind, it must have the sun or it will not live. They say that you cannot change anything except in a corresponding change of conditions. None of us would argue with science, and yet some of us have seen flowers growing in a cellar. We have seen roses blooming in December. We have seen lilies in a cesspool. The saving grace of the Lord Jesus Christ can make a person triumph over any environment.[9] Christ Jesus can take a man living "south of the tracks," in an environment of evil and corruption, and make a new man of him, victorious over his environment. We have all seen a man with the glow of God in his heart go into the downtown areas. By his preaching and living and serving the people, he wins many to a saving knowledge of Christ and grows a religious institution as God-gratifying as could be found anywhere on earth.

J. C. Lamphier of New York in 1857 went into a downtown area which had been deserted by all other churches. He began working among what was commonly called "an undesirable element." By setting up prayer meetings and by ministering to the people, he had the distinction of seeing the origin of the great revival of 1858 grow out of the church and the locality in which he labored.

There are many areas in our cities known as "static areas," areas from which the wealthier people have moved away to more desirable environments, and the poor people and those, who for the most part are not able to own their own homes, have moved in. Such areas are looked upon as static. Many churches located in these areas, where the houses are not kept painted and are not as desirable in appearance as they formerly were, have thrown up their hands, feeling that the evangelistic opportunity is too difficult and that it would be better if they were located elsewhere. However, if a church loves the lost and if its pastor will lead that church in a persistent visitation program of evangelism, these people can be won. In the areas known as static, there are still as many people living as there were in the past. They are different from the standpoint of social standing and financial ability, but their souls are just as precious in the sight of God. Some of our strongest churches today are churches which are located in such so-called static areas and have not surrendered but, through the leadership of the pastor, have looked upon the situation as a challenge.

3. Pastoral evangelism is the answer to the evangelistic needs of the growing, thriving communities on the fringes of the great cities. When the Apostle Paul entered any city, he always preached, led the people to Christ, and organized them into local churches. Of course, he would work out a plan by which they could have a pastor, as well as a group of officers, to assist in the affairs of the church. As modern cities have grown, the churches have readily taken up the idea of establishing missions in each new area, giving teachers and officers to work with that Sunday School, and finally developing it to the point where it could be organized into a full-fledged church. These young churches, located in the growing areas, are often baptizing more people year in and year out than the older churches. Young churches in new thriving areas, led by warmhearted, evangelistic pastors, are meeting a definite spiritual need. They are among the fastest growing religious groups in America today.

The evangelistic opportunities of the pastor are many and

varied. The pastor not only leads his church to win souls, but he makes use of his pastoral contacts of visiting the sick, counseling the confused, performing weddings, and conducting funerals, to capitalize on his rich opportunity to evangelize.

The Evangelistic Program of the Pastor

Every pastor will plan his evangelistic program. We rarely do the things well which we do not plan. If the pastor undertakes his evangelistic duty haphazardly and if he seeks to lead his people in a hit-or-miss way, he will never accomplish much. He must have a definite plan. The pastor's program of evangelism should consist of at least three parts: first, person-to-person soul-winning; second, revivals; and third, the teaching ministry.

1. The soul-winning program of the pastor could very well consist of two major divisions. First of all, his counseling opportunities; and in the second place, what is called "sudden evangelism." One of the most prolific soul-winning opportunities of the pastor is in the field of counseling. Often people find themselves surrounded by a chain of circumstances over which they have no control. They come to the pastor in search of a way out. Sometimes these circumstances grow out of difficulties in domestic life. Often the husband and wife are at disagreement. Sometimes they are unhappy together. There are times when parents have a very definite problem with a son or daughter, and they cannot find the answer. These opportunities afford the pastor a mighty privilege in soul-winning. Many times people come to the pastor when there are unanswered questions in their minds. One thing that the human mind cannot tolerate is an unanswered question. Often when death has taken away a loved one and the individual is left lonely, his mind will begin to explore the possibilities of life after death. In an hour of perplexity, he will come to the pastor for counsel. Often the confused individual feels his inability to cope with life.[10] The real problem generally lies in the fundamental wrongness within the individual. The person generally has a wrong relationship to God. The pastor will fail to permanently help such people if he resorts to temporary advice and admonitions alone. He ultimately must point them to faith in the living God. If he stops short of personal evangelism, he fails them.[11]

The evangelistic pastor will cultivate the unchurched people who come to him for counsel. He will not press them for a decision for Christ until he knows they are ready. He will point out their need for salvation. He will suggest certain Scriptures to be read. He may give them a small New Testament marked for their convenience. He may supply them with tracts and books designed to come to grips with their particular problems and to show them how to be saved. He will not fail to explain the plan of salvation to the lost seeker.

The pastor also will use what we call "sudden evangelism." He will talk pointedly and directly to certain lost men. He will visit them for that very purpose and after tactful introduction and approach, he will tell them their need of the Saviour and how to be saved. The pastor must do more direct evangelism than anyone in his church. If he does not seek out the lost and win them to Christ, it will be well-nigh impossible for him to lead his laymen to win the lost. Any pastor who is a true minister of the Lord Jesus Christ will never want to break with his Lord at the very center of the Lord's plan. Personal evangelism was at the center of the evangelistic plan of Christ.[12] The wise pastor-evangelist will continually watch for openings and, at the proper time, urgently press the sinner for a decision to accept Christ as Saviour. Any pastor who is gifted enough to build a sermon and to deliver it effectively has the gift of telling the story of the redeeming love of Christ for a sinful world. No professional evangelist will be able to win more men to Christ, year in and year out, than the zealous pastor-evangelist.

Dr. C. E. Matthews says every pastor should win souls for three reasons: "First, for example's sake . . .; second, for his own spiritual edification; and last, because God expects it of him."[13]

2. The pastor will plan and conduct revivals in his own church. Occasionally, he will personally do the preaching. Some feel he could do it with profit at least once each year while others think every two or three years would be wiser. He should preach in his local revivals as often as possible. The people will usually support a revival conducted by the pastor better than for anyone else. Revivals held by the pastor are often the most prolific of any held in the church. It is essential that he plan, prepare for, and lead the church in every revival effort, regardless of who does the preaching. Two or more revivals each year should be the goal of every pastor.

The evangelistic pastor will receive calls to conduct revivals in other churches. You will notice the word "conduct" is employed here. The evangelistic pastor will not merely preach in the revival, but he will promote, teach, and lead in visitation evangelism during a revival. If he preaches only, he will fail to make the necessary contributions to the campaign. In holding promotional meetings, he may go afield to personally win the lost. Every pastor should conduct some revivals beyond his own church. Our great denomination depends upon the pastors for this service. There are not enough professional evangelists to meet the demand, and if there were, it would not always be advisable to use them. We must have the touch of the man at the grassroots to balance our New Testament program of evangelism.

The pastor who engages in outside revivals will keep the fires burning in his own soul and in turn will consistently sound the note of evangelism in the regular services of his home church.[14] The church which is willing to share its pastor in this capacity with others will remain unselfish and global in its outlook. Revivals beyond his own church are good for the pastor, the churches interested, and the denomination because it makes for a vigorous and practical well-rounded program of evangelism for all concerned.

3. The pastor should conduct at least three different classes but do so only as the need arises. First, the pastor's prospect class.[15] This is a class for inquirers. These are folk who have made no public decision. These people have been discovered by alert members of the church. They may be interested but they also may be confused. They may need to know the plan of salvation or to have certain real difficulties met and discussed. The people who attend this class may be members of the Sunday School. The pastor may conduct this class during the Sunday School hour and count all present as visitors in Sunday School. Or he may conduct it one night during the week. Some evangelists urge a class like this every night during the revival.

The success of the pastor's prospect class will require the co-operation of Sunday School teachers who have unsaved people in their classes and who need special help. It is the judgment of many that all Junior and Intermediate young people who are unconverted should attend this class when the respective teachers are convinced that they are ready for this instruction. It is to be remembered that at this age youth responds readily.[16] Wise leaders will enter this open door without fail. It also requires the aid of deacons and other soul-winners and visitors in the church who are constantly on the lookout for recruits for the prospect class. The prospects will be brought to the class by those who have discovered them and by Sunday School teachers who believe that certain members of their classes are ready to attend the pastor's class. The unchurched who visit the worship services and are not connected with the Sunday School may be personally contacted by the pastor for this class.

The pastor will teach the plan of salvation. He will use the various Scripture verses which meet particular needs of those present. He will explain baptism and why the new Christian should unite with the church. He will explain why all who are saved should study the Bible, pray, and seek to improve their own lives.

Second, the class for the new converts. The pastor will go over carefully the plan of salvation to make sure all understand and that all have been truly converted. He will tell them the reasons for the existence of the church, why they have joined the church, and why they should be baptized.[17] He will show them the relationship of the church to the denomination, and its place in world missions and evangelism. He will teach the great doctrines of the faith. He will lead all in the class to tithe and will graduate them into the Training Union, Sunday School, and the WMU or Brotherhood, for a life of concerted activity and service.

Third, the pastor should teach a class for the unenlisted. Twenty-seven per cent of the resident membership of the average church is unenlisted in any of the church activities. A large percentage of the enlisted are not soul-winners. The pastor would do well to conduct a class for these two groups. He could help them rediscover the purpose of Christianity. He could point up the joy and need of witnessing. He would encourage them and create confidence in them by giving them proper instructions. Many from these groups would receive new purpose and faith from a class of this nature. Some of them would become effective witnesses.

Every new convert is a potential witness. Most of them have failed to witness for no fault of their own, but because the church did not train and use them when they were inducted into the church. All of them felt the urge and longed to tell others about their experience with Christ but did not know where to turn and what to do. After a time, the suppressed drive within them was curbed and then it died. This urge and longing is natural within the newborn Christian and may survive even after many years. The pastor's class for mature, but inactive Christians, will serve this very purpose.

The pastor, better than anyone else, may formulate a plan for contacting and enlisting these people in such a class. The matter would be too delicate to risk to anyone else. Every pastor is hopefully a diplomat. The pastor knows each member fairly well and will know how to approach him. The pastor may make special calls at the homes of these people to go over the plan for the class and ask them to visit. He may enroll them for the class while he is in their home. The pastor may get out an attractive folder advertising the class, making the class idea as attractive as possible. He should mail it to the folk with a personal letter urging them to enroll as a member. Let the folder state the time of the class, the approximate number of times it will meet, the place, and in fact, every detail about the class.

Fourth, the pastor should teach study courses. The teaching ministry of the pastor should in no wise be confined to the three classes just described, but he should also teach study courses in soul-winning in connection with the Sunday School and Training Union study courses, which will be held in his church once or twice a year. The conscientious pastor will go even further than this. He will teach as often as feasible an extra study course in soul-winning for all the members of the church. These classes will be as thoroughly and carefully prepared, planned, and advertised as are the regular study courses. He will use his sermons from Sunday to Sunday to teach the congregation. The ministry of the pastor is inescapably a teaching ministry.

CHAPTER 6

VISITATION EVANGELISM

There are two definite types of visitation evangelism. The church may choose to set aside a week for it, prepare thoroughly and put on an intensive visitation campaign, seeking to enlist and win as many members as possible. This may be done once or twice a year. The second type of visitation evangelism is perennial visitation. Through perennial visitation evangelism, the church sends its workers afield fifty-two weeks out of the year in a concerted effort to evangelize.

There are two types of visits which may be done in the perennial effort.

1. Specially trained visitors may go afield systematically to visit the people who have no contact with the church and who seem not even remotely interested. This group will do cultivative visitation. We mean by cultivative visitation that the visitors will go in and tell the people who they are, and what church they are from. They will not seek to promote the church nor the pastor, nor will they seek to get a definite decision at that time. They will talk about Jesus Christ. They will tell what Christ can do for one. They will talk about the great possibilities connected with a higher power. They will give their personal testimony, telling what Jesus has done for them. This is not a membership drive, but it is an effort to interest the disinterested in the better life. The visitors will leave a card with the picture and name of the church, the location of the church, and a cordial invitation to attend the services. This type of visitation will need considerable follow-up.

2. Specially trained visitors may make visits to definitely get decisions. If they find that it is impossible to get a healthy decision at that particular time, they, of course, will conduct themselves in such a way as to leave the door open so that they

may come back again. It is with this second type of evangelistic visitation that we shall give most of our time in this particular section.

REASONS FOR VISITATION EVANGELISM

1. Visitation evangelism is biblical. In the tenth chapter of the Gospel of Luke, we find our Lord sending out the seventy, "two and two before his face into every city and place, whither he himself would come" (Luke 10:1). He gave certain definite instructions to the seventy as to how to conduct themselves and what to say. They were to return and make a report. When they made their report, they returned with joy, saying, "Lord, even the devils are subject unto us through thy name" (Luke 10:17). Christ Himself went into the homes and talked with the people. There are at least twenty recorded incidents of Jesus' personal conversation with men and women concerning the welfare of their souls.

Visitation evangelism is also apostolic. Paul reminded the Ephesian elders of the fact that he had taught them not only publicly, but that he had gone from house to house (Acts 20:20). "Daily in the temple, and in every house, they ceased not to teach and preach Jesus Christ" (Acts 5:42). There are many references in the New Testament to this personal visitation evangelism by the followers of Christ and the apostles.

2. Large numbers of unchurched people who live all around our churches make visitation evangelism imperative. The majority of unchurched people do not attend the regular worship services of the churches. They do not attend in appreciable numbers even the great attractive evangelistic services of the most renowned evangelist. It is important, therefore, that every church adopt a system of evangelism that will reach the unchurched masses everywhere. A religious survey will often surprise the local church as to its possibilities. Dr. Dawson C. Bryan tells us of a rural pastor who was positive that there were almost no people in his particular area who were not church members. When his denomination urged every church to take a survey and join in one week's concerted visitation effort, out of loyalty to his denomination but without faith as to results, the pastor led his church to take a survey. To his utter surprise, he found eighty-six prospects living in his particular area who preferred his church. This survey was followed by a concerted visitation

effort, and thirty-eight people joined the church, twenty-one of them on confession of faith.[1]

Another church in North Dakota with a membership of two hundred and seven families made a survey of its community of about seven thousand population. The survey disclosed that one hundred and eighty-eight families preferred that particular church. The church put on a concerted visitation evangelistic effort, and within two months the minister had received one hundred and eighty-two new members into his church.[2] The people had been there all the time, but the methods used by the church had not been sufficient. Visitation evangelism is the answer. A great church in the state of Louisiana, located in a town of a little more than twelve thousand people, had won one-fifth of its entire membership within six years. The pastor had begun to feel that the field had been thoroughly evangelized until he decided to make a survey for himself. He decided to visit personally every home within five or six blocks in every direction of his church. The first afternoon's visitation was quite a revelation. Within four blocks south of the church he found more than fifty prospects for church membership. Within a stone's throw of the church were hundreds of possibilities, notwithstanding the church was extremely evangelistic. The great unreached and unchurched possibilities challenge us to do visitation evangelism.

3. Visitation evangelism uses laymen. The majority of our churches have never tapped their greatest resources for evangelism. Neither the churches nor their members are enough aware of the potential evangelistic power which the laymen can claim.[3] Most of our laymen are seldom used in evangelism. We call upon them to give, we call upon them for civic service, we place many other responsibilities upon them, but we seldom use them in evangelism. Visitation evangelism is designed for the laymen. Visitation evangelism is the only way to win the world. God has adapted it to the laymen so that all of his redeemed could have part in the redemption of the world. In visitation evangelism the churches discover their laymen and their evangelistic potential. The laymen are not only capable of going into the homes and talking about religion, but they can often do it more effectively than the ministers. Often, when the minister goes into the home, the people expect it of him. That is his profession — that is his

job. But when the layman comes into the home, they feel there must be a special interest and an unselfish reason. As Dr. George Sweazey puts it, they look upon the minister as a salesman, but they look upon the layman as a satisfied customer.[4]

Visitation evangelism is not on trial.[5] Visitation evangelism has been in use since the days of our Lord. In 1928, Dr. A. E. Kernahan decided to give visitation evangelism a thorough try-out. He went from city to city across America training laymen, sending them out, and conducting visitation campaigns in the various churches and cities. Within four years and four months he was able to see 158,109 people join the churches as a result of this visitation evangelism.[6] The laymen whom he trained and sent out were able to win on the average of sixteen converts per team per week.

At the end of a one week's concerted effort in visitation at Bedford, Massachusetts, which had been conducted by Dr. A. E. Kernahan, an elderly deacon of the Congregational church is reported to have said to Dr. Kernahan that he had been a deacon for over fifty years, and as far as he knew up until the last week, he had never been responsible for bringing one soul to Christ. But during that week his visitation teammate and he were able to win seventeen men to Christ. Now he knows that he can do this work and that this is the way that God would have us evangelize.[7]

Carlyle Brooks of DeLand, Florida, for more than forty years has visited ten thousand homes each year telling the story of Jesus to the occupants. Carlyle Brooks is almost seventy-five years old. He is still going strong and pastors of almost every evangelical denomination all over the nation are calling for his services. The writer has used him in his own church and also in evangelistic efforts elsewhere. He has never had Brother Brooks with him in a revival effort which has not been a glowing success. Often Brother Brooks has come in and reported that he has won as many as fifteen people that day, who will join the church on profession of faith tomorrow. Nine times out of ten these people have come by name and in almost the exact number which he had suggested. What Carlyle Brooks is doing in concerted visitation could be done by thousands of other laymen across America. Laymen may not be able to sing or preach or do many other religious duties, but they can do the main thing better than anyone else. They can participate in effective visitation evangelism.

The greatest hindrance to an evangelistic program is lack of faith that ordinary men can do it. The pastor does not believe that they can do it, and the laymen themselves do not believe that they can. People are generally nervous when they go out on the first or second visitation effort, but when they find how overwhelming the response is, it excites them to the extent that they look forward to the prospect of entering the next door. One layman, whose team had been instructed to pray before knocking on the door of any home, said that when they stood before the first door, he actually prayed that the folk would not be there. He has overcome that fear now because soon he was able to win several each time he went out visiting. Kernahan suggests that we do not ask the people if they can or will visit, but just tell them they have been chosen to visit, and that the pastor, the church, and God expects them to visit.[8] Many, who feel that they cannot visit and fear to try, turn out to be the most effective visitors once they have gotten into it. It is wise to place the most timid and fearful with better-trained and more effective visitors in order to convince them that it can be done, that it is a joy to do it, and that it can be done also by them. One insurance salesman, who protested the visitation effort in his church and told the pastor frankly that he would have no part in it, was persuaded to get an inside view of visitation before he thoroughly condemned it. He was persuaded to go visiting with an effective visitor. When this team entered the first home, they were able to win the entire family. They won three in the second home. They were able to win two in the third home, and when they walked out upon the street, the salesman clapped his hands and said, "This is it! This is the way to do it. This is God's plan of evangelization." Argument could not have convinced him, but an experience changed his mind. When he witnessed an effective soul-winner at work, felt the spirit of the testimony, and was moved by the response of the people, he became convinced. This particular man, working in another team, was used of God to win fifty-two people to Christ within seven days, giving only thirteen hours during the seven days to this sort of thing. Being a salesman, he knew the fundamentals of salesmanship. All he

needed was faith enough in God to believe that spiritual salesmanship can be rewarding as well as that of insurance.

4. Visitation evangelism is direct. Visitation evangelism
takes the hit-or-miss feature out of evangelism. It sends Christians out where the people are, to do a specific task.[9] The
message of the soul-winner is direct. The person who is being
addressed feels that he is being personally approached. Visitation
evangelism brings the visitor to the people. The only way to
reach the people is to go to them. The only way to reach many
people is through visitation evangelism. The very poor in the
community are not likely to attend our services because they
feel that they are too shabbily dressed.[10] Through visitation
evangelism, one is able to get into the homes of the poor, the
sick, Catholics, Jews, filling-station operators, doctors, and many
others who are employed at the very time of the regular services
of the church and who do not have an opportunity to attend the
church services.

SOME ESSENTIALS OF VISITATION EVANGELISM

1. It must be planned.[11] Every church should have a
church council of evangelism. The council of evangelism is composed of the pastor as chairman, the heads of the various departments of the church, a secretary, and as many other members as
the pastor and church feel wise to have on the committee. The
council of evangelism is not the pastor's cabinet. It is a separate
organization, whose sole duty is to plan and promote evangelism under the direction of the pastor. The church council of
evangelism will plan all of the evangelistic activities for the local
church for the entire year. They must, of course, include in this
planning the important visitation program of evangelism. If the
church does not plan a concerted program of perennial visitation,
it will most likely not prosecute this type of a program, either.

2. The program of visitation evangelism may be promoted
in three ways:

(1) From the pulpit. Announcements and comments of the
pastor will be effective.

(2) Through the weekly bulletin. Frequent references to
the evangelism program will influence the readers.

(3) By announcements and literature given out within the

departments of the Sunday School, the Training Union, the circles of the WMU, and the other lay organizations.

3. The program of visitation evangelism must be continuous and permanent. A definite time for visitation each week must be set aside.[12] A definite day will be chosen. Some churches use Wednesday in an effort to bunch the activities of the church into two or three days of the week. Most of the churches, however, use Thursday, but any day of the week that suits the particular church will be all right. The church should vote upon the day selected and set it aside, making it part of the policy of the church. Thus visitation evangelism is put on a church basis. Visitation evangelism should be done every week. The Sunday School class may choose to visit absentees who are not prospects and at the same time go further and make some evangelistic calls during the same evening. A few churches visit only once a month. This is better than no effort at all, but it is far from the most effective.

Calls are usually made during the evening, however many of the women will prefer to visit from ten o'clock until noon in the morning. Then they have a covered-dish luncheon together at which time they will make their reports. Other groups may prefer to meet at the church and go out for visitation in the afternoon. Regardless of the time selected as being most suitable, the group should always meet at the church to receive their assignments and go out for a definite time. Then they should come back to the church for reports and for testimonies.

4. Assignments must be prepared. The church council preparing the assignments will need to know who the people are to be visited and where they live. Many churches and pastors are very nebulous about their evangelistic opportunity. They will tell you that the world is their field. One's evangelistic world is no larger than the number of names of lost people which he has on cards. There may be three hundred thousand unchurched people in the city where a church is located, but the world of evangelism for that particular church consists of the number of names of these lost people which it possesses. If it has only one hundred names, then that is the limited extent of its evangelistic world.

This information may be obtained from at least five sources. In the first place, the church should take a religious census at least twice a year. It has been found that a religious census is dead with old age after six months. Nothing will bog down a program of visitation more quickly than to have the teams go to several places and not be able to find the prospects because the people have moved away. In the second place, the church will secure this information from visitors' cards signed by those who have visited the worship service of the church. It is always wise to give the guests visitors' cards. It is also necessary to remember that many people who are visiting do not sign cards. Therefore, have the church members so alerted that when one does not sign a card, he will be spoken to in a friendly way and his name and address secured before he gets out of the auditorium. An alert church will be able to do this with all ease and without any offense. In the third place, the names of prospects can be secured from the rolls of the Sunday School.[13] Through the Sunday School the church should find out how many are warm prospects for church membership. It can also find out the number of parents who are unchurched and the names of relatives of the people attending the Sunday School who live in the community but are unsaved. In the fourth place, the members of the church should be trained to watch for newcomers in their area, find out something about them, and welcome them to the community. They should find out what church, if any, they prefer, and this information should be passed on to the church council of evangelism. In the fifth place, in all large towns and cities, the Chamber of Commerce will be glad to furnish any church with the names of all newcomers. The church may visit these people to see if they are prospects. If found to be prospects, members of the church will, of course, organize to follow up the visitation and give them a cordial welcome to the church.

It is not enough to secure the names and addresses of the unchurched in preparation for the assignment. It is also vital to place on the card as much information as possible, so that the visitor may have something with which to begin. The visitor should be instructed when to return the card and how to make his report. No assignment is properly prepared or executed unless this procedure is carried out.

5. Keep the records accurately. The church council of evangelism should have a secretary who has the sole responsibility of keeping complete records and of preparing and making

assignments for visitation evangelism. If a church is strong enough, it should hire someone full-time to do this. If not, it should secure the services of someone who is apt, and, above all, who is keenly interested in evangelism. Every card on file should have several duplicates. The duplicates with proper instructions upon them will be given to the visiting laymen. The visitation card will serve a threefold purpose. It will serve as an assignment for the visitor. It will serve as a report after the contact has been made. It will indicate to the church which agency should be given credit for the visit.[14]

In order to keep the records accurately, the assignments should be classified.[15] Prospects should be classified as "warm," which means they are members of the Sunday School and have shown considerable interest. The teacher feels that they are ready for a decision, or they have been visited several times by effective visitors who feel that now these people should be pressed for a decision. Prospects may be classified also as "lukewarm." These may be people who are members of the Sunday School but have shown absolutely no interest beyond that point. Or they may be prospects for the Sunday School and have shown some interest, but have refused so far to become a part of the Sunday School, visiting only occasionally. It might also mean that they come irregularly to the preaching services of the church but seem to have very little personal interest in salvation. Prospects may be classified as "cold" or "indifferent." It is likely that this type of prospect has not attended Sunday School and seldom, if ever, attends church, showing no interest in religion whatsoever. One may be classified as a cold prospect who is cold because he has not been contacted. He is really a prospect, but nothing in particular has been done for him. His lack of interest may not be on his part, but he would still have to be classified as a "cold" prospect.

6. Visitors should be trained. It is well to guard against short cuts because they have been the ruin of us in many ways and places. At the same time the training must be simple. These people are not seminary students and will not require the same complex type of instruction. They must be given certain basic instructions. To get the program of visitation under way, the first phases of training may consist of the fundamental rules of visitation, the use of the Bible, and when and how to get a decision.

The training program will never end. Each week all visitors will be given more instruction.

The richest training is received by experience. These visitors will learn something new every day, but what they learn through experience will mean more to them than knowledge gained from any other source. We often overlook this source of training. What they get in the field of experience is not theory. It comes from the line of battle. All visitors will make mistakes, even the best trained. We must never let the fear of making mistakes drive us away from visitation evangelism. Often the sad experience of mistakes has served to be the best teacher. By serving as a teammate for several days, the most experienced visitors will show the less experienced what to avoid and how to proceed. Through observation new visitors catch the spirit of soul-winning, as well as the knowledge of methods.

Men who are concerned and dedicated to Christ, and who have good judgment, can learn enough in a brief period of study to do effective visitation. Men with limited education often do better than the most facile, who depend on their mental training. Often simple earnestness is the greatest equipment of a soul-winner. No man should demur because he is uneducated and untrained. One of the most effective soul-winners in Texas speaks poor English, but he uses what he does know with such earnestness and homespun wisdom that people forget his educational limitations and see only his great Saviour.

The training program of visitation should be continued and perfected. Often an entire week should be given purely to training. It could be in the form of a study course. The instructor would lead in a study of various types of people, the correct approach for each, and what special Scriptures to use to bring them to conviction and to a decision. The teacher should be careful to warn against the fallacy of being mechanical. He will insist on naturalness and an avoidance of a stereotyped approach. He will vary his approaches, and even dare to use unheard-of methods if the Spirit indicates.

Some Instructions for Visitors

1. Clarify in the minds of the visitors the purpose of the visit. The visitor must be led to realize that this is not a doorbell-ringing campaign, but it is a special effort to get behind closed

doors with the simple Gospel of Jesus Christ. The visit is not social. It is evangelistic. The timid and untutored visitor may be tempted to spend much of his time in talking about everything under the sun except what he came to speak of. It is a known fact that many teams never get to the subject of soul salvation or to the relation of people to God. Such a visit is futile. The visitor is an ambassador for Christ. He goes into homes to represent Christ and to speak for God. He will not be austere and straight-laced. He will be natural and at ease, but knowing the purpose of his visit, he will steadily and firmly move to his objective.

2. Prayer is essential. The team of visitors should always bow their heads and pray when they enter the car before making the very first visit. They will ask for guidance and wisdom from God. It is not enough to pray at the beginning of the evening of visitation. They must pray before they knock upon each door. Because the people in each home are different, the visitors must desire a fresh presence of the power of God for every visit. There are actually three persons on every team of visitors — the two callers and the Holy Spirit.[16] It is profitable and necessary for the visitors to have close communion with this third member of the team. While one member of the team is speaking with the prospect, the second will remain quiet and spend his time speaking to God in behalf of the one who is leading in the conversation.

When the team of visitors is deeply conscious of the presence of God and their dependence upon the power of God to the extent that they feel the need of prayer, it makes all the difference in the atmosphere of their visit as well as the effectiveness of it. It is a requirement at the seminary for all who are taking the course in personal evangelism to do personal witnessing during the course. Recently, a team of three young men related this experience to the professor. They told him how they had gone out every week for a month visiting a couple of hours each afternoon. For the first month they had failed to win anyone to Christ. Their only encouragement had been the fact that they had talked to some people, given their testimony, and given out tracts. Then it occurred to them that they had not been praying before going out upon the afternoon or evening's visitation. They decided to pray thirty minutes before each evening's visitation. The first week they did this, they were able to win two to Christ. The second week they won nine, the third week eleven, and the fourth week sixteen. They found that there was all the difference in the world. They were not only able to win men on the street who never attended a worship service, but they found it possible to win Jews, Catholics, and many others to Christ.

We have already suggested that many people, and especially inexperienced visitors, are very nervous about their first efforts. Dr. Sweazey says, "They pray better when they are frightened by the importance of what they are trying to do."[17] If visitors become sure of themselves, pray less, and lose that frightened feeling about the magnitude of their work, they will lose their effectiveness.

3. The situation must be favorable for a visit. The visit must not be made standing on the doorsteps or outside the door of a home. The visitor must get into the house. If he is not invited in, then tactfully he should ask if he may come in a few minutes to talk to the family. If then he does not receive an invitation, he will excuse himself and pass on to the next visit. The visitor will never represent Christ and never pursue his call standing outside the door. Set the family at ease with a greeting of friendliness that will reveal to the people that you are a down-to-earth individual. When the visitor first enters the home, ordinarily he is a stranger and there will be a bit of stiffness in the atmosphere. Unless he begins with a friendly greeting, this stiffness may intensify. If the visitor shows a sincere interest in the home, the people are likely to respond.[18] If the wife and children are already members of the church, in eighty per cent of the cases it would be far better to speak to the husband and father alone. Many visitors will go in and greet the people warmly and then ask for a private conference with the man. Or they will ask him to come with them for a ride and will talk to him in the car. Often wives with the best intentions and the most sincere concern will say the very wrong thing at the wrong time. If the visitor is certain of the temperament of the wife and is not afraid of interruption, then it would be better to speak to the husband in the presence of the wife. If the entire family is unchurched, it is far better to speak to all of them at the same time.

If there are distractions in the room, remove them. If the

radio or the television is being used, it may be well to ask, "Is this your favorite program?" If it is not the favorite program, someone will possibly take the hint and turn it off. If it is not the favorite program and it is not turned off, ask if it would be all right to discontinue the program. If the program is one of their favorites, then excuse yourself and make a date to return at a later hour. The environment for an effective visit must be correct.

4. Speak the language of the people. Steer away from "preachy" expressions. If the prospect is a mechanic, talk in terms of a mechanic. If he is a farmer, use language and illustrations which are familiar to him. If he is a professor or student, you may be more technical. Never ask him, "Are you saved?"[19] If he has a church background, he will possibly understand the visitor; but if he has no religious background whatsoever, he will not understand. Our Saviour never used this type of language. Meet the prospect on the level of his interest and operate on the plane of life which is familiar to him. Evangelistic terms and religious phraseology may defeat your purpose.

5. Use of the Bible. The visitors should always carry a small New Testament or a small Bible with them. Do not carry a large Bible. The very sight of a large Bible under the arm of a visitor may prejudice the prospect immediately, or it may cause him to unnecessarily throw up his guard. No one appreciates religion on parade. People would rather see it in the heart. It is well to carry a small Bible in the purse or shirt pocket. The average visitor would do well to confine his Scriptures to two or three simple passages which exactly fit the individual's case. It is confusing to turn continually through the Bible and read a large number of Scriptures. Stay with one or two passages, repeat them, explain them, and use them until they have penetrated into the heart of the individual. The Bible is the sword of the Holy Spirit. He blesses its use by the soul-winner. There can be no conviction without the use of the Bible, but the Holy Spirit must be present to make it effective.

6. Certain mistakes to avoid in visitation.

(1) Do not argue. People are not won by argument. They are set in their ways. Bitterness and hatred are generally stirred up. All men resent being outdone or out-argued. The visitor is a bearer of an invitation. He invites people to a better life. He

invites them to a great institution. Most important of all, he invites them to a Saviour and to a saving relationship in the family of God. He has nothing to argue about, but something great to positively present. If the people argue, detour them. If they persist in argument, diplomatically excuse yourself and pass on to a visit that may be more effective.

(2) Do not get frustrated. Some will manifest hostility. Some will immediately offer opposition. The visitor must always be kind. He must never lose his poise. He may be able to influence more by the kindly attitude he displays, than by any statement he could make. The most debased and twisted mind in people can recognize the difference between a spirit of magnitude and one which is puny and cramped.

(3) Do not lose your temper. No matter what anyone may say or what he may do, keep sweet. When you leave, thank him kindly for admitting you to his home, tell him how you appreciate the opportunity of conversation with him, and invite him to church.

(4) Do not become discouraged. Often visitors have gone out on rainy or cold, snowy nights to operate against the odds. They have talked with the people. They have left decision cards and come back cold and discouraged, feeling that the visit was futile. They found out within a few weeks that several people united with the church as a result of their concerted effort. Archibald says, "No one fails in this work except the one who does not make the attempt."[20]

(5) Do not be detoured. Sometimes the people visited will bring up for discussion theological questions and questions with religious tainted labels; such as, predestination, infant baptism, or which church is right. The wise soul-winner will not go into a discussion of these matters. He will inform the individual that these matters are important and should be discussed, but not until one is in position to understand the spiritual implications. One who is not a Christian and who has not accepted the fundamental principles of the Christian religion is not ready to go off into such details. The visitor will not be detoured therefore but will continue with the main issues, such as how to be saved. Every soul-winner has seen the attitude of the argumentative on controversial, theological subjects radically changed after the prospect has had an experience of grace with Christ. One

man persisted in arguing about baptism. He said that he had already been christened into some organization, and therefore it was futile for him to consider baptism again. The visitor would not discuss the matter with him. Instead, he tactfully asked leading questions and found out that the man had never had a definite experience of regeneration with Christ. Therefore, he majored upon this subject, and when the man finally came to accept Christ as his personal Saviour, the question of baptism was rightly solved.

(6) Do not ask for a decision too soon. Many a heart is weary and hurt and must have the Lord's touch. The visitor should never run ahead of the Lord or the prospect. Some of these people are stubborn; some of them are in deep sin; they need to be free from the bondage of sin. They have been many years getting into this condition. Therefore, it will take patience, time, and the truth of God to deliver them.

(7) Make the visit brief and with purpose. No visit should be long. If the people are not prospects, the visit should not last over three or four minutes. If they are warm prospects, the work can be done and the decision can be made within a brief time. The average visit should certainly not extend beyond twenty or thirty minutes at the most. If the visitor is not able to secure a decision within twenty or thirty minutes, he should break off but leave the door open so he may return at another time to take up the conversation and carry forward to conclusion.

(8) Always give the visitors a brief, mimeographed instruction sheet. It will be impossible for any group of visitors to remember all of the important things which the leader will say to them before they go out on the visit. Take every precaution. Mimeograph the important things in brief form. Ask them to review this sheet before they get into their car for the evening's visitation. Ask them to turn to it again and again when they stand before doors, and when they are uncertain as to what to do.

(9) Instruct the visitor as to how to get a decision. There are times when it is unwise to press for a decision even though the prospect is warm. Often, however, it is necessary to do so. Getting a decision is an important phase of visitation evangelism. The difference between success and failure often lies at this point. After a visitor has had some experience, he will generally know how to proceed. When the plan of salvation has been

explained and the prospect thoroughly understands it, they may bow for prayer and the visitor may pray earnestly for the salvation of the prospect. Then call upon him to pray. If he cannot pray, dictate a prayer, expression by expression, and have the prospect repeat after you. Often in the course of this prayer, God does His work. Sometimes this may not be a wise procedure and should not be done. The prospect should be urged to sign a decision card if the decision is genuine. If he will not sign the card, you may explain it to him again, leaving the card with him, and coming back for another visit at a proper time. It is possible for a life-changing decision to take place during one visit and often it does. God is wonderful. His power is amazing. The human heart is remarkable. The God who made us can do anything with us. Every experienced soul-winner has seen men, women, and children make decisions for Christ the very first time they were ever approached on the matter. These decisions were genuine and the life lived afterwards proved it.

CHAPTER 7

EDUCATIONAL EVANGELISM

Educational evangelism is an organized effort to enlist and train church members. It also provides organizational outreach for evangelism. It would train Christians to witness, and it would bring the unchurched into the Bible study program and confront them with Christ as Saviour. It is neither an extensive training program which seeks to educate and culture folk into the family of God, nor an effort to find God by understanding His laws of human growth and development. Nor is it a process of bringing one into oneness with God in Christ. We recognize that every person must have certain knowledge before he can be saved. He must recognize his need of a Saviour, who the Saviour is, and how to receive Him. Men are not saved by the teaching process, but the teaching process prepares men for a saving experience with God. Educational evangelism is not opposed to sudden conversion, but conversion is preceded by some instruction.

Christianity is a crisis religion. A crisis arises in every life at conversion. There is always a crisis when Satan is overthrown in a life, and the Prince of Peace is installed as King. One does not always need a long course of instruction before conversion, but after conversion the instruction must be vigorous and cover a long period. Educational evangelism is an endless process which begins before conversion and continues until death. "Education means the development of a kind of person."[1] In educational evangelism it means the development of a Christian. Educational evangelism does not operate on the philosophy that all are naturally the children of God and that the only need is to develop the good within. Educational evangelism is dedicated to completing the work begun in conversion. It is a matter of record that all groups which have defined educational evangelism as a training process which brings people into a union with

God without a transforming experience have steadily declined.[2] This type of educational evangelism is not an effective ingathering process. But vigorous educational evangelism, with the twofold aim of bringing all people everywhere under the influence of the Gospel and of training the converted, is of paramount importance in the twentieth century.

It is our purpose to give careful study to the place of the Bible school and the training organization of the church, in educational evangelism.

THE SUNDAY SCHOOL

The most effective method in evangelism in the twentieth century is the Sunday school. Evangelical churches today are effective in evangelism in proportion to the type and size of their Bible schools. The churches which are reaching their respective communities evangelistically and are building large memberships have live, growing Sunday Schools.

1. The Bible school is an enlistment agent. In the majority of cases, eighty per cent of all converts come through the Sunday School. It should be the contact agency of the church. All ages and types of people are visited and enrolled in the Bible school. Here their hearts are warmed with Bible teaching. They are then led to remain for worship. They are brought into the Bible school, worship service, Christ, and church membership. As Dr. Short points out, the church school remains a continuing contact point for all its people.[3] There is a place in the Bible school for all members of the church, regardless of age or spiritual background.

2. The Bible school is an evangelizing agent. Among Southern Baptists only twenty per cent of the converts are won apart from the activity of the Sunday School. This points up the value of the Sunday School in soul-winning. All other efforts in evangelism reach only one-fifth of the total number evangelized. Many evangelistic techniques are used by the Sunday School, such as visitation, personal work, group evangelism, and in fact almost every method known to us. However, the Sunday School could be far more evangelistic. It is reported that eighty per cent of all people enrolled in evangelical Sunday Schools pass through without being converted.[4] Among Southern Baptists the per-

centage is slightly smaller. They actually win about thirty-three per cent of those enrolled. This number, however, accounts for eighty per cent of all their converts. The ratio of conversions each year has been in direct proportion to the enlargement and efficiency of the Sunday Schools.

The importance of the Sunday School in evangelism cannot be overemphasized. In the city of Dallas, Texas, are many great evangelistic churches. We shall refer to two of them, but not by name for obvious reasons. About the turn of the century, both of them called as respective pastors two of the greatest pulpiteers of that generation. One of these churches saw the value of the Sunday School in reaching the people, while the other gave emphasis almost entirely to the pulpit ministry and power of evangelizing at the preaching hours only. Fifty years later, the two churches are still serving in their respective areas of the city. The church that saw the value of building a great Sunday School, as well as emphasizing the pulpit ministry, has 11,000 members with 6,000 enrolled in Sunday School and an average attendance of 3,500. This church has also mothered a large number of other churches which are now also influential institutions. The church which failed to see the value of the Bible school as an enlistment and evangelistic agent has today a membership of 1,300 with 575 in attendance in its Bible school. It has led in the establishment of less than a half-dozen other churches. Both churches are sound in the faith. Humanly speaking, the difference in accomplishment was due to method.

The Sunday School as an evangelistic agent was first used extensively in America by John Mason Peck on the frontier in 1817.[5] Peck, a young Baptist preacher, was sent out by the American Baptists. He organized many local Sunday Schools, developed them into missions, and they finally grew into full-fledged churches. He organized these Sunday Schools into associations for the promotion of better evangelizing techniques and for spiritual inspiration. In this way the Sunday School held a strategic place in frontier life. D. L. Moody also was a strong believer in the Sunday School as an evangelizing agent. He would train his new converts and give them classes to teach. If there was no class for the convert, he would urge him to contact people and organize a new Bible class.

The Aim of the Sunday School

The aim of the Sunday School reveals its place in evangelism. Its aim is not to enroll numbers for numbers' sake. The school is concerned with numbers only because they represent people being reached for God. Neither is the Sunday School concerned merely with lesson teaching. All people need more knowledge about Christianity, but the work of the Bible school is not just to feed hungry minds with religious truth.

1. The first aim of the Bible school is to teach men the way to God. The Bible teaching about salvation should be clearly presented. The teacher and class should work for the commitment of the unsaved to Christ.

2. The second aim is to teach the Bible so as to build Christian character. This type of teaching will develop the new Christian into a strong, well-rounded personality. Paul urged as much upon the church at Ephesus when he said, "and he gave some, apostles . . . and teachers; for the perfecting of the saints, for the work of the ministry, for the edifying of the body of Christ" (Eph. 4:11-12). The body of Christ must be edified as well as redeemed. A redeemed soul needs the milk of the Word. Effective evangelism will nurture as well as give birth to its children.

How to Build and Use an Evangelistic Sunday School

1. The general and department officers of the Sunday School must be compassionate of heart and trained in mind. A staff of officers committed to soul-winning and willing to learn how to create an evangelistic atmosphere in the organization of the Sunday School will develop an evangelistic Sunday School.

The chief superintendent must be selected on the basis of his ability to lead in constructing an evangelistic organization.[6] The wise pastor will constantly look for superintendent timber within his membership. He will counsel with such men, train them, and have them chosen first as department superintendents. He will gradually season and ripen them for the important office of chief superintendency. He will not wait until he needs such an officer, to begin searching for him. He will have several ready and waiting at the time of need.

(1) The chief superintendent's relation to the school.[7] He will develop an evangelistic atmosphere by his example as a

soul-winner. He will encourage each teacher to cultivate the lost in his class and win them to Christ. He will promote and conduct study courses in soul-winning to meet the needs.

(2) His relation to the department officers of the school. He will require all department officers to attend weekly teachers' meetings. He will provide a competent teacher to teach the following Sunday's lesson, always giving the lesson an evangelistic slant. Everyone connected with the school should hear the lesson taught. The only time this can be done for the teachers and department officers is at the weekly teachers' meeting. There can be no evangelism apart from constant, prayerful study of the Bible. Department officers are as responsible for winning souls as are the regular teachers. The superintendent will urge that all department officers avail themselves of the opportunity to hear the Bible lesson on Wednesday night as well as join in a visitation program.

(3) His relation to the teachers. He will meet often with all the teachers by departments. He will take the lead in discussing the spiritual status of the school and the particular needs of each department. He will check on what is being done evangelistically and will offer positive suggestions suitable to each department. He will furnish the teachers with the best literature on evangelism, including tracts on soul-winning.

(4) His relation to the individuals in the school. He will keep a close check on all the pupils in the school. He will have a list of every unchurched family and individual enrolled in the school. He will use this list to accomplish two vital things. First, he will work for the total enlistment of every church member into the complete life of the church. He will enroll them in courses in soul-winning. He will find a niche of service for every saved person in his school. In the second place, he will know the names and some facts about every unchurched person in the school. He will visit and deal personally with all possible and will employ help to assist the teachers in reaching others.

(5) His relation to the pastor. He will confer with the pastor and the church council of evangelism concerning plans for the Bible school and will present these plans to the officers and teachers of the school. He should be an elected officer of the church and will always work in conjunction with the pastor and the church council on evangelism.

The department officers must be chosen with great care and led to a practice of fruitful evangelism. The department superintendent and the associate may well hold the key to the evangelistic outlook of the entire department.

The department superintendent should meet the same qualifications as the general superintendent, and his relation to the department should be similar.

The membership associate holds a strategic place evangelistically. This officer has much to do with the visitation program and enlargement of the school. He keeps up-to-date lists of names for visitation, which he has received from the secretary of the council on evangelism. He assigns these names to the teachers and classes. He is responsible for having the visits made within the prescribed time limits and the names and information returned to the council secretary for reclassification or reassignment.

2. The teacher must have a consuming desire to see every unsaved person in his class committed to the Saviour.

(1) He must be concerned.

(2) The teacher must be burdened with the condition of the lost. He must be convinced that every lost person is under the wrath of God (John 3:36). He must lead the pupil to realize his condition before God (John 3:18).

(3) Every teacher must have a burning passion for the lost. The driving urge within will then compel him to approach the unconverted in his class.

(4) He must realize his personal responsibility to bring the unsaved to the Master.

(5) He must depend completely on God.

(6) If the unsaved pupil is a Junior or Intermediate, the teacher must seek to help, instruct, and guide the parents in their counseling with the child. If the parents are ignorant of the spiritual needs of the child or if they are indifferent, the teacher must know what to do to win the parents. To be compassionate is not enough. The teacher must know the solutions for the common evangelistic problems. He must have good common sense and patience, coupled with knowledge.

The teacher is the point of contact with the pupil.[8] The ultimate aim of all Bible-school teaching is to bring the pupil **into correct relation** to God. If the teacher is convinced of this, Sunday school evangelism is made easier. If the teacher is uninformed or indifferent at this point, it will be difficult for the pastor and the superintendent to accomplish effective evangelism in that class. The teacher has access to the home which few others have. He can prosecute a thoroughgoing program of from class-to-home and from home-to-class evangelism without making it obtrusive. If all Bible-class teachers could be brought to see their opportunity and do perennial evangelism, there would be no need of special decision days in the school. The teacher, if open-eyed, active and consecrated, may be able to win for Christ all the lost in his class, as well as the parents and relatives of the pupils. If he accomplishes that, he will not excuse himself from further evangelistic activity. He will enlist still others into the membership of his class or will assist other teachers in evangelizing the lost in their respective classes. The teacher must realize that a converted member is not thoroughly evangelized just because he has accepted Christ and has united with the church. He must teach and guide the convert as to Christian character and Christian principles. He must, therefore, have a well-rounded conception of Bible teaching.

3. The text used by the church school is essential. The Bible must be the textbook. The teachers will use any sound material available to make their teaching more Christ-centered and helpful, but the Bible will remain the basis of their teaching.

The teacher must know the Bible as a whole, and not merely as isolated fragments. The Bible must be used in the class. Often neither the teacher nor the pupils bring their Bibles to class. Literature is valuable but should in no case take the place of the Bible. "Often the key to the lesson does not lie in the text which is on the lesson leaf, but in the context which could be profitably studied if the teacher and class had their Bibles in hand."[9] It is good for the teacher to teach with his Bible in his hand. It creates a love for the Book and adds authority to what is said. Often the Bible is misjudged and has had almost nothing to do with the life of Sunday School pupils, all because it was not really *the* text of the school.

The teacher need not be too concerned with current events, world politics, and psychology. If the Bible is the textbook, the lost will be converted, the saved will be made strong. Luther, Calvin, Augustine, and almost all great men of God were converted after they came into contact with His Word. No Sunday school has ever been evangelistic which has used substitute materials for the bulk of its curriculum. Our teaching must be Bible-centered as well as Christ-centered.

4. The Sunday school must have a definite plan of evangelism.

(1) Designate certain Sundays when certain departments of the Sunday school will sit in a body at the morning worship hour. Begin with the Juniors and include in order all departments of the school. Recognize the department by teachers and classes at the worship hour. Keep this program going all year. It will do two things. First, it will bring the unchurched under the power of the Gospel. Second, it will help form the habit of attendance at worship. Each time a department remains in a body, a few will be awakened to the need of remaining for worship each Lord's Day.

(2) Use group evangelism. Hold "decision day" at least twice each year for each department. An excellent time is during the revival effort sponsored by the church. These decision days should be prepared for. They must be well planned. The teachers will slant all lessons toward the decision day for at least six weeks in advance. The teachers will also speak personally to individuals who they feel are ready to decide for Christ. The departments and classes will prepare the atmosphere by much prayer and concern. At the department meetings for teachers and officers, the teachers may present the names of the lost for special prayer. A concerted visitation effort will be put forth to have all present who should make decisions.

The opportunity for decision will not be confined to the unchurched only, but an appeal for dedication of life or for special service will be made to all. The appeal for special service may be made in all departments above the Junior ages. A special decision card made out by the local church should be used. These decision days, however, should never disintegrate into merely a lifting-of-the-hand and signing proposition. There must be a clear-cut, down-the-aisle stand for Christ. Proper planning and careful direction under the guidance of the Holy Spirit will safeguard the service.

When decision days are conducted for the Juniors, Intermediates, and Young People, the level of the service must always be spiritual and not emotional. Mass psychology must be carefully avoided. The decision must be as individual as possible. It is easy to have a landslide of youth in such a service which, if encouraged, may lead to superficial conversion. Sob stories should not be tolerated. Explain the plan of salvation and urge the youth to respond. Do not pressure them.

The individual church will decide what disposition to make of the decisions. No evangelist would presume to tell the church what it should do, but it has been the experience of most of us that the new convert should be received as a candidate for church membership. This does not mean that he becomes then and there a member, but he will be received as a candidate only. Then the pastor will meet with those making decisions and teach them what it means to become a Christian and what it means to join a church. After the pastor has become convinced that the candidate is ready to be inducted into the church, he will baptize him into the fellowship of the church. Then the new member will continue in the pastor's class for further vital instruction before he is graduated into the various training organizations of the church.

(3) Weekly visitation by the Sunday School. This program of visitation will be thoroughly explained in a subsequent chapter.

(4) From the Junior and Intermediate departments, the teachers may bring interested young people to the pastor's office by appointment. Invite one or both of the parents to witness the meeting. The pastor will explain the plan of salvation and help the interested youth to make a decision. This is a most wholesome plan. The soul-winning is done by the best authority in a spiritual atmosphere and in the presence of the finest audience, the loved ones.

(5) The Sunday School should conduct an enlargement effort each year.

A Soul-Winning Training Union

It should be the ultimate aim of every organization of a New Testament church to win souls. The purpose of the Training Union is to train for effective church membership. No church member is effective who does not participate in this main task of every Christian. We are never to substitute other church work for soul-winning. The Master admonished His followers to "bear much fruit" (John 15:8). The Training Union could be to the Sunday evening worship service what the Bible school is to the morning worship. It could build the evening attendance and create an evangelistic atmosphere for soul-winning. The evening preaching service could be a great hour for evangelism. If the attendance is poor and the unchurched few, it will be an ineffective and disappointing service. All churches which consistently enjoy excellent Sunday night attendance are churches with healthy and adequate training organizations. If the Training Union made no other contribution than building a great evening attendance, it would be worth all any church could put into it.

Dr. R. O. Feather says, "a parallel study of the growth of Training Union work and the number of baptisms reported each year by Southern Baptist churches reveals the influence of Training Union on baptisms."[10] Dr. Feather's statement can be proved by the records, but the Training Union is not the bridge between the church and the world outside. That function belongs more to the Sunday School and Brotherhood than to the Training Union. The evangelistic function of the Training Union is peculiar and quite distinct. It is the bridge between the responsibility of the church to win the lost and the great host within the church membership who have no sense of obligation in personal witnessing nor any idea as to how to begin. Thousands who never think of attending church will permit their children to attend Sunday school. By and by the Sunday School forces will be able to win to Christ these children and their parents. The laymen's organization will be able to lead business men, who would never think of attending church otherwise, to attend a church supper, hear a brief religious address, and feel the warmth of Christian fellowship.[11] In this manner the lay organization serves as an introduction to the Gospel for men of the world. The Training Union backs up the Sunday school and Brotherhood by training people to perform such vital and major tasks. The Training Union will enlist and help train that group of unenlisted and unrelated church members for effective service in all other organizations.

Dr. J. N. Barnette points out how any church can win one person to Christ for every eight church members on the rolls of the church, "by bringing the Sunday school enrolment to exceed by 25 per cent the total church membership, and by enlisting the entire church membership in the Training Union."[12]

Why Use the Training Union in Soul-Winning

1. In order to harness youthful zest and extra energy for the greatest cause on earth. The world bids for our youth. Political philosophies and ideals clamor for youth. Nazism used young people to spearhead its drive in Germany. Communism is capitalizing on the strength of youth. Crime, with its false promises of excitement and profit, bids for young people. The majority of all the crimes committed today are committed by youth. Youth thrills great crowds every season in all types of athletics. War marches on the feet, and flies on the wings, of youth. Many churches are giving too little attention to youth, except to criticize them for their participation in the world about them. The churches, which do not provide wholesome outlets for the energy of youth and do not seek to employ their brains and zest in building a healthy fiber of society, have no right to complain if the growing generation indulges in the questionable practices of society.

Young people are enthusiastic by nature. This enthusiasm is not unnatural nor a thing to be curbed. It is to be used for good. As men grow older they tend to lose their enthusiasm. Older men ripen in judgment but become less agile. The church needs both enthusiasm and judgment. If it employs its young people with middle-aged and older folk in soul-winning, it will have a strong combination of energy and common sense working for it. It has been the experience of most leaders that it is as easy to lead young folk into serious activity as it is to enlist them into the light and frivolous. Young people have lofty ideals and are prone to be true to and serve them better than are more mature Christians. History records that the majority of the great soul-winners and mighty religious leaders began while very young. Count Zinzendorf was only twenty-seven years of age when he became the guiding light of the Moravians. John and Charles Wesley were Oxford youths. George Whitefield swept two continents toward God before he was twenty-five. Charles Haddon Spurgeon was nineteen when he captured London. Hundreds of others could be recalled from the pages of history made golden by the eternal thread of youth.

2. As a preventative measure. Here a negative approach becomes a positive reason. There is but a thin line between positive goodness and the path to shady practices. If our less mature Christians are recruited for vigorous testimony, it will prevent them from becoming entangled in sinful activities which always beckon. If one's mind and hands are busy with divine duties, he will not be easily led astray. Active people of all ages are happy and growing people. To lead young people to win souls not only prevents them from being caught easily in the snares of sin, but it deepens their faith and lessens their doubts.

3. Because it capitalizes on youth psychology. There is a strong group psychology among Intermediates. They fear what the group thinks more than they fear Satan. Each wants to be a regular fellow. The wise church will not ignore this fact. Though conformity per se is not good, the church will hurry to go through this open door. Intermediate young folk have influence with each other that no one else has. If a few key members can be contacted and led to consecrate themselves to soul-winning, the entire group may be led to win souls. No spiritual force is more potent than a group of youths on the march for Christ. The church must see this and capture the ship of youth. If the church permits itself to be pushed aside by the public school, worldly pleasure, and everything else, it will not appeal to its youth. Happy is the church which is awake and aggressive enough to capitalize on its youth and employ them in soul-winning. This cannot be accomplished by opposing most of the things which claim the attention of the young people nor by browbeating them. The church must aggressively and winsomely step forward to get and appreciate their co-operation in the big task of soul-winning. Youth can be challenged by the church, but they will not be caught in the snare of coercion.

4. The future of the church. Up to this point the discussion has centered around youth. It is well to remember that at least fifty per cent of the Training Union enrolment should be adults. The church is responsible for enlisting every member in its training program, regardless of age or background. The training organization affords training for those who need it, and a job as a leader or teacher for those who are ready and qualified to

train others. The experienced soul-winners find in the Training Union a prolific field of service. They can stimulate and guide inexperienced soul-winners. They can be used in showing the beginners how to exercise the fine art of discipling. If the main purpose of the Training Union is to train an effective church membership, then the very first training obligation is to teach Christians how to win souls. The future of the church depends on its attitude toward, and its participation in, evangelism.

How to Lead Training Union Members to Win Souls

The approach will depend on the age group involved. The church will use one approach for its youth and another for the adults.

How to Lead the Youth to Witness

1. Begin with something which appeals to young people and absorb them in the will of God. Begin with something they know and like. The program must meet two needs. Young people must be consecrated and they must be trained for witnessing. To set a date for a study course and announce the course to be taught at the church is not enough. Why not rent a camp ground near the city? As soon as school is out, let the church sponsor a summer camp for the Intermediate young people for one week and the Junior groups at another time. Keep expenses to a minimum by urging sponsors and leaders to go along and help. Plan a full program of activity for each day. Let the day's activity include in the early morning a sunrise worship, breakfast, study, lunch; in the afternoon, rest, play, and a campfire consecration service after supper. Here you meet the youth on their own level of thinking and challenge them with study and consecration services. Build all the study around soul-winning and let each campfire service be prepared to deepen the spiritual life. The church that does this will find its young people returning from camp trained and consecrated and ready to be directed in witnessing by the training organizations.

2. Give them wise, alert, and consecrated leadership. For Juniors, almost any consecrated adult will do as long as he is deeply interested in the work. For leaders of Intermediates, more is required than just consecration. These leaders must be neat in appearance, as well educated as possible, and holy in character. Employ no leader for them, however winsome and

attractive, unless he is clean in conduct and noble in purpose. Long-faced, sanctimonious people will not do. Leaders must be clean and holy, but also full of sunshine and optimism. If the church can find and train such leaders who at the same time love the lost and are eager to win souls, it is well on its way to leading its youth to witness effectively for Christ.

3. Generate spiritual atmosphere in the Training Union and worship services. The church which totally ignores the social element makes a sad mistake, but the church which thinks it can enlist its youth and hold them with pink tea parties and whoopee is blind. There is a serious side to youth. It is the deeper side. They are serious about almost everything. They go about their play, love, or war, in a serious tone. Try giving them a spiritual atmosphere and see what happens. Religious life for youth built on the frivolous is not conducive to witnessing. There is no point in gathering a hundred young folk in an organization each Sunday night unless they are thereby brought closer to God and guided into positive service for the Lord.

4. Use the youth in special evangelistic services. Begin by sending them out, properly chaperoned, to other churches to give programs. Encourage them to sign and distribute tracts in street services, jails, etc. At least once each year conduct a youth-led revival in the church. This effort must be well advertised, properly organized, and adequately sponsored. Let the youth work alongside all other members; each will participate in the visitation program of the church. Train and expect the youth to do personal work in all group efforts in evangelism sponsored by the church.

How to Lead the Adults in the Training Union to Witness

1. Let the training organization sponsor a soul-winning study course at least once each year. The church council of evangelism, in co-operation with the officers of the training organization, should pledge all possible to take the study course.

2. Each week the organization should do visitation evangelism under the direction of the church council of evangelism.

3. The members of the Training Union should be urged to work each week in conjunction with the Sunday School as it visits the unchurched and seeks to lead them to a decision for Christ.

4. Committee activity affords one of the greatest opportun-

ities for development in Training Union work for adults and young people. Every Training Union member above the Primary department is responsible for committee activity. The committee personnel should be changed every six months to give to all a variety of training. These committees are so designed as to cover every phase of local church life.[13]

The missionary committee will compile the names of unsaved folk from the religious census and rolls of the Sunday School and assign them to the proper age groups in the Training Union for evangelistic visitation. All such activity will be under the direct supervision of the church council of evangelism, which will co-ordinate the witness activity of all church groups.

CHAPTER 8

PREPARATION AND PERFORMANCE IN REVIVAL

One cannot prepare for revival without considering methods. Some will say, "God wants better men, not better methods." If we knew the exact wishes of God, we might find that He is concerned about both. Better Christians are basic in God's plan, but goodness does not eliminate the need for implementation. The fertile soil of California is capable of producing excellent fruit; but first, fruit trees must be planted and cultivated. After these trees produce luscious fruit, it must be distributed to the consumers everywhere. All the elements for production are there, but implementation is necessary. Better Christians who are instructed and guided will be used of God more effectively in evangelism. Fresh ways of making the Gospel of Christ real are vital.

Dr. C. E. Matthews has often declared that "preparation is seventy per cent of the success of the revival crusade."[1] All who have had experience in conducting revival crusades will agree that this statement is true. In a revival the evangelist may sow seeds of the Gospel and break up new ground, but his main task is to reap. Revival time is harvest time. If the ground has not already been broken, the seed planted, the proper cultivation and season provided, no rich ingatherings can be expected. Long and thorough preparation is essential.

There are two types of preparation. They are: organizational and spiritual. One may go to the extreme in either direction. We may place all emphasis upon spiritual preparation and not succeed; or, on the other hand, we may place all emphasis upon organizational preparation and thoroughly fail. It is too often the case that we thoroughly organize but fail to provide the necessary spiritual atmosphere. This is always a grave mistake and has been the occasion for much criticism of organizational preparation.

ORGANIZATIONAL PREPARATION

1. It is necessary to take and use a census. There may be thousands of unchurched persons living in the locality of the church. Unless the church knows the names and addresses of these people and something about them, it is not likely that it will reach them. We may feel that the whole world is our diocese, but the people whose names and addresses we have on cards at our disposal constitute the size of our evangelistic world. It will not be our purpose to discuss in detail the religious census, inasmuch as a thorough and excellent discussion of the religious census is given in the *Southern Baptist Program of Evangelism* by Dr. C. E. Matthews, beginning on page 56. Every religious leader should know how to set up an associational organization for taking a religious census. He should also know how to actually take the census and direct the people in using the information secured. If the census data is thoroughly taken, properly distributed, assorted, graded, tabulated, and assigned, it becomes one of the most vital instruments in the hands of the church to evangelize.

2. Publicity. The great industries spend multimillions of dollars each year in publicity. They say that the first nineteen times a product is advertised on radio, television or the newspapers, it seems to make almost no impression upon the public. But after the nineteenth time it begins to have cumulative effect, and the product begins to move with ever increasing volume. If this is true with industries and with the products that people need, how much more important it is for the Christian church to know the value of publicity and how to use it well. If the average business concern used the same advertising techniques which are employed by the average church, it would have to go out of business within less than a year. Often the church will buy one or two small advertisements in the paper and possibly a spot announcement or two on the radio. When the world does not stick its head into that church auditorium to see what is going on, then the church is led to think that publicity is fruitless. Through efficient publicity, the church is able to get the attention of the world and to create a desire on the part of the people to come to the church to hear the Gospel.

It is not enough to thoroughly advertise and to create an avalanche of interest, but this interest must be heightened as the revival continues, and to do so, publicity must continue. The Coca-Cola Company says that when they cease to advertise for as few as three days, the sales of Coca-Cola fall off noticeably in that particular area. If this is true of a well-known, well-publicized item, then of course one can readily see the value of continuing to publicize any product, whether it be spiritual or material.

Publicity has always been necessary. John Wesley believed and practiced thorough advertisement. Wesley lived in a day when publicity was little known and little used, and yet he thoroughly advertised his meetings and campaigns. Charles G. Finney believed in and used religious publicity. He was severely criticized in his day by the Calvinists for his methods of publicity. Just as it paid off for John Wesley, it also blessed the efforts of Charles G. Finney. Dr. W. E. Biederwolf said, "The devil comes along with something the natural man wants, and he paints the town red to let them know he is coming. The church comes along with something the natural man doesn't want, and thousands of pastors seem to think a mere announcement of the project from the pulpit is quite enough."[2]

General Booth of Salvation Army fame often advertised his meetings. On one occasion he advertised that a reclaimed gambler, a saved woman from the streets, and a converted drunkard would tell what Christ had done for them. This publicity filled the entire auditorium to overflowing.[3]

The primary purpose of such publicity is to create within the people a desire to come to the revival services. To accomplish this, the publicity must be properly circulated. There should be a capable committee on publicity, who will decide on a type of advertisement, which is attractive and easily read.

The second purpose of revival publicity is to popularize the meeting.[4] There are certain preferred media of publicity. First, newspaper ads are possibly one of the best means. It is never wise to buy a large ad. It is always better to buy several small ones, one column in width by three inches long. Scatter these small ads all through the paper for several days rather than buy large ads every two or three days. In the second place, radio and television have proven to give some of the very best religious publicity. A fifteen-minute program on the radio every day for the duration of the revival effort or a few fifteen-minute programs on television will do much to capture the attention of the community. Many churches have used effectively street streamers, billboards, handbills, storewindow cards, sidewalk signs, streetcar signs, car-bumper cards, and cards for visitors to hand out up and down the streets and in the homes of the people.

Brief newspaper reports of the services publicize a revival well. Someone who knows how to write such reports can easily make a news item out of each service and get it to the publishers. The newspapers always welcome news items if they are well written. Only those versed in journalism and familiar with newspaper composition should attempt to write up the daily reports of the revival.

3. Train visitors and personal workers for the revival effort. If a church has a concerted visitation program, it will already have its visitors trained, will use them, and will select others to go with those already trained. If the church does not have such a program, a study course to train those who are to be used in the special visitation effort before and during the revival must be set up. Newly enlisted visitors must be taught how to get into the homes and what to say after they are in. Each team must carry publicity of the revival to hand out in every home which they visit. They should urge upon those visited to meet them at the revival service; or, in some instances, they will get the people to agree to be taken to the services.

Effective quick training for prospective visitors for a revival effort can be given through a showing of an excellent film on visitation and soul-winning. When the moving picture is finished, go over the ground covered by the picture and explain it. Have prospective visitors take notes both on what is in the picture and what you say to them by way of explanation. It would be fruitful to follow the film and brief lecture with testimonies from experienced visitors.

4. There should be at least two banquets the week prior to the revival. All the workers and visitors of the church will come together. At this time assignments will be given out and the people will be organized into teams. If the community is large enough and the possibilities are sufficient, it would be well the first night to major on visitation to detached church members. At the close of the supper and assignments, a short inspirational message with last-minute instructions on how to make a

brief and effective visit should be given. Then the teams should be sent out immediately for at least one hour or an hour and a half of concerted visitation. They should seek to pledge every detached church member to join the church during the revival, preferably the first day of the revival. If a concerted effort of this kind were put forth in every revival conducted by every church throughout the land, many of the millions of detached members would be enrolled in church membership in the community where they reside.

The visitor should be instructed as to what to say to these detached church members. Among the instructions they should be informed to tell them that a revival meeting is beginning in the local church or in the church nearby. Also that it is the duty and privilege of every Christian to be a member of the church in the area where he lives that he may be of service. Try to pledge them to unite with the church the very first service of the revival. Tell them that a goal has been set; that, for instance, the church has set a goal of fifty detached church members to unite with the church at the very first service. Tell them that they have plenty of company, and that as they walk the aisle for God, many others will be doing likewise. If the church can begin its revival effort with a large number of unaffiliated church members coming into the active membership of the church, it will give quite a spiritual impetus to the revival as well as bring these people out of idleness and lethargy into usefulness and a sense of responsibility. This particular banquet should possibly be held on a Tuesday night. Then on the following Thursday night the second banquet should be held.

At the second banquet the same workers and visitors will assemble. They will be given different instructions. They will be sent out in teams nearly the same as before, but this time they will be given the names of lost people. Each team should be given from two to four names but not more than four. They should be instructed to spend as much time as necessary in each home to talk about the church, to magnify Christ, to explain the plan of salvation, to give their testimony as to what Christ has done for them, and to urge these unsaved to accept Christ and to commit themselves to Him. If they are successful in securing a commitment, then those committed should be asked to sign a commitment card. The team of visitors should try to get the committed person to agree as to just exactly what service he will attend and when he will make his decision. If necessary, make a date to bring him to the church for the services.

There is a third type of meeting which may be held the second week of the revival. This would be a luncheon or supper meeting for businessmen. Each Christian businessman would bring some non-Christian to the meeting at which time a well-prepared meal would be served and kind, warm friendship would be demonstrated. A brief speech on the value of the church and on Christ as Saviour should be given by someone who knows how to make such a speech. This should be followed by two or more vibrant testimonies — testimonies given by businessmen who have found the Lord, who have joined the church, and who can tell in a few brief words what it means to them.

5. At least three months before the initial day of the revival, a study of the great revivals of the past should be taken up. It would be a rewarding exercise to do this every Wednesday night, studying one of the great revivals each night. Give the date of the revival, the type of revival, something about its leaders, and the particular technique used. Acquaint the congregation with the great personalities whom God used in the revival. Quote excerpts from the accounts and make that particular revival live again. One may begin by studying first the revivals of the Old Testament; then follow with one or two of the revivals of the New Testament; and finally conclude with a thorough study of the revivals of later history.

Excellent books to be used in preparation for such a study are: *Old Time Revivals* by John Shearer; *Revivalism in America* by W. W. Sweet; *Evangelized America* by Loud; *A History of Evangelism in the United States* by W. L. Muncy, Jr.; *Revival of Religion in England in the Eighteenth Century* by John S. Simon; and *Revivals in the Midst of the Years* by B. R. Lacy.

A thorough study of the revivals of the past every Wednesday night for three months, and then at the end of each meeting having the people get upon their knees to call upon God to send a revival after the order of one of those studied, will help to bring a revival to the church. In almost every place where this has been thoroughly done, long before the end of three months, revival fires have been known to crackle in the church and souls walk the aisles. There is something strange and powerful about the study of the great demonstrations of the power of God among His people in the past. This was one of the first methods used to teach evangelism in the schools in the early days of our nation.

6. Give personal assignments to responsible people several weeks before the revival begins. An excellent system, which this writer has tried, has been to select from twenty to fifty of the consecrated members of the church. Call them for a meeting immediately after the morning preaching service about three weeks before the revival is to begin. In this meeting, give each one of them a sealed envelope with the name and address of a lost person enclosed. Ask them to pray about these names for at least three days before breaking the seal, then open the envelope and see for whom they have been praying. Next they should visit these unsaved persons, get acquainted with them, cultivate them, have them in their homes and bring them to the preaching service as soon as possible so that their hearts may be warmed. Many of these people will join the church in the very first days of the revival. It has been recorded that some of them have found the will of God for their lives before the revival days began.

Another rewarding method is to assign to a consecrated family an unchurched family. Have this family befriend the unchurched family, invite them into their home, bring them to church, and eventually talk religion with them, giving them tracts that explain the plan of salvation and the reasons for joining the church. Have their hearts warm and their minds receptive for the early days of the revival. Have a supper at the church on Tuesday night, when each family will bring the family with whom it has been working. At that meeting, the pastor and evangelist will speak briefly on the plan of salvation and other words of helpfulness. Then each family will sit with its prospect family in the services and pray for them that they may make decisions even in that very service.

SPIRITUAL PREPARATION

Without spiritual preparation all organizational preparation will be of no avail.

1. Deepen the spiritual life of the people. When the members of a church become more aware and acutely conscious of

God, their spiritual life will be deepened. People will become aware of God when they are led to pray. Therefore, it is imperative that the people be urged to pray. "The greatest things in existence will only be given to those who pray."[5] Too often we feel that the greatest things in religion can be accomplished only by passionate preaching, or magnificent singing, or by personal effort of some kind. The greatest things in existence will be given only to those who pray until the windows of heaven are opened and God pours out the victory through the Holy Spirit.

Prayer is the life of religion.[6] Prayer is talking directly and face to face with God. It is speaking to God as a son speaks to his father. When one prays he has fellowship with God. He speaks out of his heart to God whom he feels to be very near.

Dr. R. A. Torrey gives a prescription for revival. He says this prescription will bring revival to any church or community on earth. One of the ingredients in his prescription for revival is prayer. His total prescription is, "First, let a few Christians (there may not be many) get thoroughly right with God themselves. This is the prime essential. If this is not done, the rest, I am sorry to say, will come to nothing. Second, let them bind themselves together to pray for revival until God opens the heavens and comes down. Third, let them put themselves at the disposal of God to use them as He sees fit in winning others to Christ. That is all. This is sure to bring a revival to any church or community. I have given this prescription around the world. It has been taken by many churches and communities and in no instance has it ever failed and it cannot fail."[7]

Often we must organize for prayer to get the people started. This is not merely a need and a characteristic of our age; it has always been true. The great frontier revival, beginning about 1800, began after letters had been sent out by the Presbyterians to all denominations in 1795, urging the people to pray on a special day — on the first Tuesday of every quarter.[8] In Logan county, Kentucky, in 1799, James McGready, pastor of the Red River and Jasper River Churches, pledged his people to pray, and they met for prayer and fasting every third Saturday. They followed this later with sunrise prayer meetings and twilight prayer meetings. It was only after these organized efforts for prayer that people began to pray spontaneously, and the revival broke out.[9] The same thing was true with the Great Revival of 1858. It began as an organized prayer meeting under the leadership of Jeremiah Lamphier of New York City.[10]

(1) The individual should be led to pray. It may be well to prepare cards and place them in the hands of the members of the church. Have them write the names of certain people for whom they will pledge to pray and urge upon them to pray daily for these particular people. It may be well to lead the individual to sign a pledge card to pray daily for revival in general.

(2) Lead individuals to pray in groups. One of the most effective group prayer meetings is the neighborhood prayer meeting. Select homes suitably located in the church community and conduct neighborhood prayer meetings in these homes beginning from one month to two weeks prior to the revival effort. Train the people who are to conduct these services. They should be instructed to lead an inspiring song service, read the Scripture, bring a brief message on the plan of salvation, and spend some time in hearing testimonies. Pray for the unchurched and for the revival. A particular Sunday School class, Training Union, or some other unit of the church should be assigned to each home to visit and urge upon the people to attend the neighborhood service, to provide chairs, songbooks, and testimonies. These particular groups may be assigned permanently to one location or may be switched about from week to week or from night to night. Many unchurched will visit a neighbor for a prayer service who would not think of going to a regular church service. When they have felt the warmth of the service, listened to the good singing, heard the natural, sincere testimonies, listened to the direct message of the leader, and the prayers of earnest people, their hearts will be warmed. Many of them will follow the group next Sunday to church. The neighborhood service not only creates a spirit of prayer and brings down the power of God; it also prepares individuals for decision when the revival begins.

Another worthwhile technique in group prayer is the all-day prayer meeting at the church. Set aside a certain day for prayer at the church. The people will be asked to come for thirty-minute periods, bow their heads, read the Bible, and pray for at least thirty minutes in the church. This is often done on Satur-

days prior to the revival and during the revival. It is always wise
to conduct all-night prayer meetings. One should organize for
these prayer meetings. Do it by departments in the Sunday
School or use any of the organizations of the church which are
suitable. Many have found out by experience that the majority
of the people are more or less straight-jacketed by present-day
society. Unless we are able to cut across the grain and induce
the people to pray and think on matters of Christianity, they
will not participate sufficiently in the revival effort to see real
revival.

Many churches have used the prayer-partner idea very
effectively among young people and women. Teams of two will
be formed and these individuals will pray simultaneously each
day. At least once a week they will meet together to kneel and
pray for the revival.

All the people should be urged to pray in their homes. Urge
the families to read the Scriptures and pray together for revival.
If many churches today have lost their power, it is certainly not
the fault of God. God is as powerful now and as willing to ad-
minister His convicting regenerating power as ever before. The
God of Luther and John Knox, the God of Richard Baxter and
Latimer, the God of John Wesley, Whitefield, Gilbert Tennent,
and Jonathan Edwards is still on His throne and He is as ready to
bless us with revival as He was these men. When we meet the
spiritual conditions, God will bless our efforts.

2. Lead the people to great concern. When the Christian
becomes genuinely concerned, the sinner can also be led to
concern. "For as soon as Zion travailed, she brought forth her
children" (Isa. 66:8). The proper atmosphere must exist before
souls can be born into the family of God. Concern is one of the
vital elements of this atmosphere. There must be travail. Someone must be gravely concerned. Christians must be willing to
match their blood and sweat with the sacrifice of Christ upon
the Cross.

There is no real evidence of deep concern among God's
people today. All would like to see a revival and all would enjoy
the refreshing gales of the Spirit, but very few seem to be
concerned sufficiently to meet the condition. Who stays awake
all night now because of the lost? Who prays all night long as
did David Brainerd, the missionary among the Indians in the

days of the Great Awakening? Who weeps over the multimillions in sin, stupidity, and ignorance, on their way to eternal perdition? If we are not gravely concerned, why not? Could it be because the rich truths and promises of the Bible are not real to us? Could it be that we do not have the same conviction of the destiny of men that Jesus, Simon Peter, Paul, and others had? Has the flame been quenched in our hearts because of intellectual attitudes? When there is unconcern, there is always a reason. I am not sure that anyone could define the reason today, but we may do well to emulate the example of men like B. H. Carroll and Charles G. Finney.

Dr. B. H. Carroll, the founder of Southwestern Baptist Theological Seminary in Fort Worth, Texas, who prayed that his last breath be an evangelistic breath, conducted a revival in Belton, Texas. The great crowds came to hear him. They always came to hear him preach because of the relevancy of his message. The people were interested and greatly inspired by his dynamic message, but, night after night, there seemed to be no concern. The results were negligible. Dr. Carroll became so intensely burdened that he could not sleep. Finally, one night he got up and walked down the highway to a cemetery on the side of a hill, about a mile from the city. He walked into the cemetery and got upon his knees and began to pray. He cried out of an anxious heart, "Lord, if you have called me to preach, I want you to show me what hell is like." That night God pulled back the curtains and revealed afresh to the devout preacher the destiny of lost men. As he preached the next night, he said it seemed to him that the flames of hell leaped up into his face, and he preached as a dying man on his way to hell. God used him to stir concern in the hearts of the audience and the people responded in a marvelous way.[11]

3. There must be complete surrender.[12] Jesus told the rich young ruler, "Go and sell that thou hast" (Matt. 19:21). When the young man heard what Jesus said, he went away with a sorrowful heart because he had great possessions. He was not willing to surrender everything. These words were spoken by the Lord to a man under conviction who stood in need of salvation, but these words are also directed to the Christian. If the Christian would see revival, he must surrender all. He must

place everything upon the altar before God. He must be willing and ready to go everywhere seeking souls.

It is not enough that the Christian surrender his love for the world and his alliances with things that are earthly, but he must surrender to the world-wide task of winning souls. He must surrender himself to the tremendous joy of Bible reading and Bible study. Revival almost always begins in the heart of some Christian and spreads rapidly to the hearts of others, until great numbers are engulfed in the mighty grip of spiritual concern.

4.   Lead the people to read the Bible. In any period when the Bible is read and studied carefully, revival fires will burn. From the pages of the Holy Book, the very hand of God will reach up to take hold of the heartstrings of those who read, to lift them, to inspire them, and to fortify them for whatever task He has in mind.

History is replete with illustrations of how revival has come when people rediscover the Word of God. In the seventh century B.C., a great revival came to the people of God under the leadership of Josiah. This particular revival came when Hilkiah the priest and Shaphan the scribe brought the book of the law to the attention of the king and, "it came to pass, when the king had heard the words of the book of the law, that he rent his clothes," saying, "Go ye, enquire of the LORD for me, and for the people, and for all Judah, concerning the words of this book that is found: for great is the wrath of the LORD that is kindled against us, because our fathers have not hearkened unto the words of this book, to do according unto all that which is written concerning us" (II Kings 22:11, 13). After this, the king gathered all Judah and Jerusalem together and "he read in their ears all the words of the book of the covenant which was found in the house of the LORD" (II Kings 23:2). When this was done, great revival came to the people of Judah.

The knowledge of the law convicted the people of sin, and when they were convicted of sin, they turned to Jehovah for salvation.

Other excellent illustrations are found in the books of Ezra and Nehemiah. The eighth chapter of Nehemiah records how all the people were gathered together before the water gate. Ezra, the priest, brought the law before the congregation, both men and women, and from a wooden pulpit in the center of the street, read from the Word of God. From morning until midday Ezra and his assistants not only read from the Word of God, but they caused the people to understand the law. When the people heard the reading of the law and the explanation thereof, they were penitent. They realized their guilt before God. Realizing their guilt, they repented, and because of repentance God was able to forgive them and bestow upon them great rejoicing.

At Pentecost the Apostle Peter quoted from the prophets and preached Jesus to them, using the prophetic statements as the basis for his message. When Savonarola stood up in the cathedral at Florence in the Middle Ages and read and expounded the prophets, great spiritual awakening came to the city. When Martin Luther and his compatriots preached the Christ of the Old Testament and the New Testament as the Saviour of men, great revival came to the land. No wiser thing could be done than for the leaders to create within the hearts of the people a desire to read the Word of God, and then to lead the people to systematically study the golden pages of the inspired Book.

PERFORMANCE IN REVIVAL

Performance in revival will consist of: preaching, praying, singing, visitation, and promotion. Methods vary, but principles are constant. Types of preaching and methods of visitation will change, but underlying principles of these performances will remain.

1. Evangelistic preaching. Preaching is of major importance in revival. There have been a few revivals in which preaching was not prominent, but these have been very few. There has never been one in which there was no preaching. The revival of 1858 and the Welch revival are generally referred to as great revivals without preaching; but we must not forget that great preachers like Charles G. Finney, Jacob Knapp, Theodore Cuyler, Henry Ward Beecher, and many hundreds of others preached daily with all their strength during the revival of 1858. The preaching of Evan Roberts in the Welch revival may have been disorganized and only a testimony, but it was charged with spiritual power and greatly used of God.

Evangelistic preaching may be topical, expository, textual, and in fact may fit into any classification; but it must be positive, simple, direct, and searching. It must bring the people face to face with God's claims, warnings, and promises.

(1) Evangelistic preaching is positive.[13] The emphasis is never on the negative. It is not a series of moral axioms, but a series of gospel facts. When Peter and John were used to heal the impotent man at the Gate Beautiful, a great crowd of amazed people gathered about them in Solomon's Court. Simon preached an evangelistic sermon (Acts 3:12-26). The sermon consisted of a series of gospel facts. The subject was "Christ" (Acts 3:12-13). The body of the message stressed three facts: (a) the death of Christ (Acts 3:15); (b) the resurrection of Christ (Acts 3:15); (c) the need to repent (Acts 3:19). He concluded with an exhortation (Acts 3:25-56). The entire emphasis was positive. It got results. The effect is seen in the large number of conversions (Acts 4:4), and the reaction of the Sanhedrin (Acts 4:2).

(2) Evangelistic preaching is searching. It reaches the conscience. It brings men face to face with God, with themselves, and with their needs. It lays bare the soul. It discovers sin in the life. It is convincing. When Paul and Barnabas entered Iconium, they visited the synagogue and "so spake, that a great multitude both of the Jews and also of the Greeks believed" (Acts 14:1). They spoke convincingly. What they had to say was searching and impressive. As a result it brought conviction and was used of God.

(3) Evangelistic preaching is simple. To be plain and easily understood is not to be shallow. It requires better thinking and much more study to make the message simple than to appear deep and profound. Simplicity is an evidence of work and much study. The simple message will appeal to the great mass of ordinary folk. It is popular in style. Jesus was a popular preacher because the common people understood Him. Worthy illustrations will help clarify as well as capture and hold attention. Too many illustrations may have a weakening effect on the Gospel, but a few well-chosen human interest stories will greatly assist.

(4) Evangelistic preaching is scriptural. The Gospel is "the power of God unto salvation" (Rom. 1:16). What the preacher says, regardless of how logical and dynamic, will not be as effective as the Word of God. The Word of God is the source of

faith (Rom. 10:17) and not the clever words of man. The Word of God is the hammer that breaks (Jer. 23:29). "The word of God is quick, and powerful" (Heb. 4:12).

(5) The content of evangelistic preaching. Effective evangelistic preaching deals with sin, the cross, resurrection, judgment, hell, heaven, repentance, faith, and salvation. Christ is the subject of the Gospel. When one preaches on sin, he will always do it in the light of Christ and show how sin alienates man from Christ. Every phase of the Gospel is enunciated in its relation to the Christ. The judgment, hell, heaven, repentance, and faith have no meaning apart from Christ. Often these basic and fundamental subjects are used in a harmful way because they are not properly related to the love of God which drew salvation's plan and to the Christ who is the heart of the plan.

2. Evangelistic singing is an essential performance in revival. At least fifty per cent of the time allotted for the service should be given to singing. Singing is not a preliminary part of the service; it is not an effort to get folks ready for the main thing, but it is part of the main worship. The Gospel in song is as sacred and effective as the Gospel in sermon. Often the singing will get through to some people who could not be touched by any other part of the service.

(1) The type of music needed for a revival is gospel songs. All uplifting church music is inspiring and conducive to worship. The anthem has always been used with mighty effect, but for revival services it is wise to sing only gospel hymns. Sing familiar hymns. Never try to teach the congregation a new song in a revival service. Some singers use choruses or introduce a new chorus or two in the course of a revival campaign and it does not seem to hinder. But to seek to teach new hymns as a rule is not effective.

(2) All should sing in a revival service. The leader and choir will lead, but the entire congregation should be encouraged to enter into the service. When people participate in a service, they become a part of it, their hearts are mellowed, their minds are opened, and they are ready for effective gospel truth.

(3) The purpose of revival singing is to prepare the hearts of the people for God to speak to them. A stirring song service will brighten the atmosphere and will warm and integrate the crowd into a congregation of worshipers. The song service creates

an atmosphere in which a sermon may be born. To preach to a cold, unrelated crowd is a heart-wearying task. Preachers will never know until they get to heaven how much they owe song leaders and choirs for the effectiveness of their sermons. The pastor, evangelist, and song leader constitute a team. Each is dependent on the other, and the entire service depends on the teamwork of all three. This writer has never worked with a singer who wouldn't co-operate. They are, for the most part, a spiritual group of dedicated men. The main purpose of evangelistic singing in a revival is to get decision. The best singers will begin with bright, lively singing. They will help the service to deepen as it moves along and prepare the atmosphere for decision.

3. Prayer in revival. If prayer is indispensable in preparation for revival, it is even more essential that prayer be continued throughout the period of the revival effort. The first great revival of Christianity had its origin in a prayer meeting. "These all continued with one accord in prayer and supplication" (Acts 1:14). The second chapter of Acts reveals the detailed results of that outstanding prayer meeting. Once the revival began, the devil answered with persecution. The devil is always ready to fight the cause of Christ. Peter and John were arrested (Acts 4:3). After the trial by the Sanhedrin, the two disciples were let go. When they returned to their own company, they reported their experience with the Jewish court and told of the threat of the court "and when they heard that, they lifted up their voice to God," and said, "now, Lord, behold their threatenings: and grant unto thy servants, that with all boldness they may speak thy word" (Acts 4:24, 29). If they had not continued to pray, the revival wave would have abated. Nothing feeds the flame of revival like prayer. Genuine, Spirit-filled revivals cannot begin without prayer, nor can they continue without it.

Promote prayer by preaching on it during the revival. Call for special periods of prayer. Sometimes it is effective to have an all-night prayer meeting right in the middle of a revival. Hold up certain prayer statements, such as are found in Jeremiah 33:3 and John 14:14, and challenge the people to claim these promises. It may be well to adopt a prayer promise for the revival and constantly urge the folk to pray with one hand on the promise and the other in the hand of God.

4. Visitation in revival. This is not intended to be an exhaustive treatment of method in revival, but only a few suggestions at the best. An exhaustive treatment of revival visitation may be found in the *Southern Baptist Program of Evangelism,* page 125. Visitation is essential to a successful revival. Visitation is seldom spontaneous. It must be promoted. Methods will change from time to time. Often a method will wear threadbare but the principle lives on. We are continually discarding old methods of visitation evangelism in revival and instituting fresh ideas. For the last five years such techniques as the pack-the-pew, prospect dinner, Bible school at night, and many others have been used effectively in many areas. Any method which enlists church members in a concerted visitation program will greatly enhance the revival.

In addition to the methods suggested in the *Southern Baptist Program of Evangelism* some have found it a rewarding practice to meet on Friday evening after church with the new members who have joined the church since the revival began. Remind them that each one has a loved one or a very close friend who believes in him and with whom he possibly has more influence than anyone else. Get them to discuss this and to mention the names of some of these people. Then urge them to spend part of Saturday visiting these particular people, urging them to come to church with them on Sunday morning. Many of them may be converted in the Sunday morning service. Those who are not prepared or ready for a conversion may be visited Sunday afternoon by the pastor and the friend of the individual who invited him to church that morning. In this way many new people for Christ will be reached, enabling the revival to conclude with a greater number of accessions; and the new convert will be initiated as a soul-winner.

It is well to meet with the young folk on Saturday and lay the revival afresh on their hearts. Tell them what to do for the Sunday services. Give them a program of visitation and a program of prayer. Make them responsible for a special service the second week of the meeting. Young people will be able to reach other young people whom no adult could possibly reach. In a revival we must marshal all the forces of the church and continue to use them.

5. Promotion in revival. The pastor will promote the revival

from the platform during the regular services and through the church bulletin. The publicity committee will keep before the community the progress of the revival by furnishing the newspapers with readable reports. The evangelist will use at least three minutes each night to emphasize a vital phase of the revival and certain services. Any service especially promoted will be better attended than one which is not. The heads of the organizations of the church will keep the meeting before their respective groups. They will do this to keep interest high, to keep each group in touch with the revival, and to keep them working in the revival.

Chapter 9

EVANGELISTIC INVITATION

Every revival service and almost every worship service should conclude with an invitation.[1] We mean by invitation simply inviting men to accept the Saviour. In this chapter we shall deal with the public invitation. The nature and method of the invitation may slightly vary with the section of the country and the local church. For instance, in Cuba one would never invite people to become Christians, for they believe if one is a human being, he is a Christian. But if a man is urged to become a "believer" in Cuba he will recognize immediately the significance and grasp the meaning of your invitation. Generally, throughout America we (Baptists) publicly urge folk in the invitation to come forward professing Christ as Saviour. This is possibly because we have taught our people to expect it.

The public invitation is not given in most places in Europe and Asia as we give it in America because the people have not been taught to expect it, and many pastors do not know how. Often American evangelists bring about embarrassment by attempting to superimpose a fixed technique upon the pastors and people in these lands.

Many of our leaders have referred to the invitation as "drawing the net."[2] Others prefer to refrain from the use of this expression because it seems to infer coercion, or the process of taking by force the good along with the bad. When a soul-winner urges a man to accept the Saviour, he is only an instrument in the hands of the Holy Spirit. He does not really draw a net, but he pleads with the man to voluntarily embrace Christ as redeemer.

WHY GIVE AN INVITATION?

There are too many reasons to enter into a full discussion here, but we must consider several impressive arguments for the public invitation.

1. The first reason for giving an invitation lies in the danger of otherwise frustrating those who hear the preacher preach for a verdict without providing an opportunity for commitment.[3] Commitment is the purpose of the invitation. It would be well to thoroughly understand what is meant by commitment. Dr. Elmer Homrighausen, Professor of Christian Education in Princeton University, has given us some choice thoughts. "Decision means bringing the discussion to an end in favor of one side or the other . . . it cleaves life in twain . . . it is not casual. It dethrones man and puts Christ in command of life."[4] Commitment goes further. It "pledges a line of action."[5] Decision declares that it is in favor of certain action, but commitment pledges itself to the action. Repentance is closely connected with decision and commitment.[6] In repentance, the center of life is shifted. It is shifted from self to God, from egotism to altruism, from sin and rebellion to a saving relation to the Saviour. The repentant person thus possesses the proper attitude for spiritual re-creation. The preached Word of God creates faith (Rom. 10:17). This is part of the work of the enabling grace of God. Without the grace of God no man could decide to commit himself to the Saviour. When God's grace works faith and repentance within a man, he should be given a chance to follow through and publicly commit himself to Almighty God.

2. The invitation should be given to complete the gospel message. The invitation is the climax to the sermon.[7] The invitation is not something tacked on to the end of the sermon. The burden of the soul is not delivered until the preacher urges men to come to Christ.[8] If a man goes fishing in the gulf and after great expense and patience gets a strike and reels the mighty leviathan up to the side of the boat, he would not think of throwing line, tackle, fish, and all back into the deep and rowing to shore. That would be the last thing to cross his mind. However, that is just exactly what a preacher does when he preaches a sermon and fails to press for a decision. People are moved and inwardly cry out, "What must we do?" In the invitation we answer the inquiry of the hungry soul.

It is not fair to God, who trusted the Gospel to us, when we fail to ask men to decide. It is not fair to the people who have visited, prayed, and worked for the service. It is unfair to the lost who listen to the instructions in our sermons and then are not given a chance publicly to commit themselves.

3. Give the invitation to get decision. The difference between success and failure in evangelism often lies just here.[9] It is not how well the soul-winner can present the truth, nor how forceful his sermons are, but how adept he is in leading the lost to decide for Christ, that determines his degree of success. The purpose of the evangelism of Jesus was to save the lost. "For the Son of man is come to seek and to save that which was lost" (Luke 19:10). It is not enough to instruct the lost and warn them of the impending doom, but they must be persuaded. Paul said, "Knowing therefore the terror of the Lord, we persuade men" (II Cor. 5:11). Before every sermon the evangelist should reconsider both his motive and object. If the object of the message is to please, or merely to inform, it should be changed. Every sentence and every paragraph should pull for a decision.

4. Give the invitation to ripen the fruit. Most evangelists begin extending the invitation in the very first service of a revival effort. Often men will be moved in the invitation who had not been touched in the body of the sermon. During the pleadings of the invitation song and the exhortation of the preacher, the Holy Spirit is able to prepare hearts for a decision, which may be made in a later service. Every professional evangelist and pastor-evangelist has had men who responded in one service tell him that they were really converted in a previous service. During the invitation the lost are brought face to face with the Holy Spirit and His convicting power. Charles H. Spurgeon was brought to Christ by an invitation extended by a lay preacher of the Methodist church. The layman was uneducated, his sermon was worse than poor, but he urged the audience to look to Jesus. He shocked Spurgeon by shouting to him, "Young man, look to Jesus!" He looked to Jesus and was saved. If that Methodist layman had not given that invitation, Spurgeon might have remained lost.[10] It was an invitation given by an uneducated Methodist preacher that led this writer to decide for Christ. He was saved then and there, but he went out into the woods to seek the face of God. Out there alone in the forest, he found peace with God through Jesus Christ His Son.

5. The Bible is replete with calls, appeals, and pleadings for men to come to God. In many of the cases in Scripture, the

exact idea of the present-day type of invitation is not intended, but the germinal idea is there. In some cases the basis for the modern invitation is there beyond any doubt. In the thirty-second chapter of Exodus, after Moses came back from Mount Sinai and found the people lapsed into idolatry, Moses invited them to declare themselves for Jehovah. It was a clear call to a public stand on the side of the Lord. He did not have in mind the same objective which we have today when we urge men to come out on the Lord's side, but the basis for the idea is present in the incident. When the people of Joshua's generation had gone into idolatry, he called on them to "choose you this day whom ye will serve; whether the gods which your fathers served that were on the other side of the flood, or the gods of the Amorites, in whose land ye dwell: but as for me and my house, we will serve the LORD" (Josh. 24:15). This was a plea to choose between the Lord and the gods of the heathen. This is akin to the invitation Moses gave at Sinai. It is personal, and it tells us that God used men in the early centuries to publicly plead with the rebellious to forsake evil and turn to Jehovah. Elijah gave an invitation on Mount Carmel nine hundred years before Christ by urging the fearful crowd to stop halting between two opinions and serve the God who answers. The people responded to his invitation when they saw a demonstration of the presence and power of God.

Peter gave the invitation as the climax to his great sermon at Pentecost. Peter had delivered the body of his sermon and had reached the climax which is described in the following words, "and with many other words did he testify and exhort." His invitation may have contained as many words and illustrations as the body of the sermon. The length of the time of pleading is not the point, but the fact that he actually exhorted the people to act upon what they had heard is very significant. Peter was as much under the direction of the Holy Spirit while he exhorted as when he preached. The evangelist is not pushing the Holy Spirit aside when he pleads in the invitation any more than when he prepares and delivers the body of the sermon. He does brush the Holy Spirit aside if he resorts to tricks and traps by which he seeks to pressure the audience into a premature decision. The honest preacher will use the invitation to help men decide for God, but he will not ensnare the people into moves which are unreal and are products of fleshly agitation. The evangelistic invitation is a form of persuasion, but it is persuasion carefully guarded by the Holy Spirit. The evangelist must ever remain mindful that he is persuading men in the power of the Holy Spirit to accept Christ as Saviour. The evangelist must hide behind the Cross and must not be seen then nor afterward.

6. The invitation is historical. Through the succeeding centuries representatives of Christ have in one form or another publicly urged men to respond to the Gospel. Those who preach for a verdict also call for a decision.[11] From the first-century followers of Christ until the evangelical revival, we know very little about the type of public invitation used by men who preached for a verdict. In keeping with the conception of missions and evangelism which was prevalent in those centuries, and with the practical polity of the churches, there was no place for a public decision. All children of believing parents were baptized into the church. To be a member of the particular nation seemed to make one a Christian. Since there was no need for a public invitation, it was not practical. Ambrose won Augustine to Christ, but it was not by public decision. As late as the seventeenth century, Richard Baxter was used to convert almost all the people of Kidderminster, but he had the families come one family at a time to his home where he talked to the entire family for at least one hour. Following that, he would take each member of the family aside and talk personally with him.[12] He used this type of personal evangelism to supplement pulpit ministry.

It must be remembered that if a pastor fails to invite his listeners to accept Christ he is departing from the practice of the New Testament church. The church at Jerusalem gave an invitation through Simon Peter on the day of Pentecost, and "there were added unto them about three thousand souls" (Acts 2:41). The practice of adding thus to the church did not discontinue with Pentecost, for later Luke records, "And the Lord added to the church daily such as should be saved" (Acts 2:47). Let it also be remembered that a departure from the use of the invitation was in keeping with the perverted notion of missions and evangelism which prevailed in those centuries. In these centuries when the practice of invitation was discontinued, it was held that missions and evangelism were a commission only for the early disciples. It was commonly believed that in baptism one was converted. This baptism was not believers' baptism but the baptism of infants.

The practice of giving a public invitation was revived and given widespread use in the Great Awakening and the evangelical revivals. While Jonathan Edwards, George Whitefield, Theodore Frelinghuysen, Gilbert Tennent, et al., preached in America, John Wesley and his followers preached for a public verdict in England. Within six months Jonathan Edwards received into his church in 1734 almost all the adult population in Northampton, Massachusetts. Whitefield, both in England and America, preached to great crowds, and many were converted. We do not have a record of the type of invitation which was used at first in the Great Awakening, but we know John Wesley used the "mourner's bench" in the evangelical revival. The "altar call" was an extended invitation to respond by coming forward and kneeling at the altar in the front of the auditorium. Here at the altar penitent sinners were prayed for and counseled. They were exhorted to come forward while the congregation sang. Often at the end of each verse a long exhortation was given.[13]

John McGee, a Methodist preacher, gives an account of the type of public exhortation used at the Red River Revival in 1799. He said, "William [his preacher brother] felt such a power come over him that he quit his seat and sat on the floor of the pulpit. . . . There was a solemn weeping all over the house. At length I rose up and exhorted them to let the Lord God Omnipotent reign in their hearts and submit to Him and their souls should live. . . . I left the pulpit and went through the audience shouting and exhorting with all possible ecstasy and energy, and the floor was soon covered with the slain."[14]

In 1801, Elder Lemuel Burkitt, from Kehukee Baptist Association in North Carolina, visited the revival which was being led by James McGready in Kentucky. When he returned and told how over six thousand had been converted and baptized within six months, the majority of the churches in Kehukee Association were greatly revived. Revival proportions were reached in Kehukee Association in 1802. During this revival period the preachers would pass up and down the aisles after the sermon, shaking hands in a friendly way with many. Then the preachers would invite all who felt themselves lost and condemned to come down near the platform and kneel for prayer.[15] From thirty to three hundred often would come forward. The churches would receive converts for baptism during the conference of the local church. The conferences were always open assemblies. Often the converts would relate their experiences and many were converted because of the testimonies.

In 1817, Asahel Nettleton began the use of the inquiry room in connection with his "anxious meetings."[16] The inquiry room gave him a chance to separate those under conviction from the rest of the congregation in order to properly instruct them. In the inquiry room individuals could speak with others without the excitement and pressure of the crowd.

At Rochester, New York, in 1830, Charles G. Finney introduced the "anxious bench" as it was then called. It later was called the "anxious seat." All who were under conviction were urged to come forward and sit in a certain section down front reserved for the convicted. The preacher would often speak directly to them during the sermon and would meet with them in an after-meeting. The "anxious bench" was one of the new measures so opposed by hundreds of his contemporaries.

7. The invitation has been used in various ways across the years. Charles Spurgeon, the great Baptist preacher in London, England, would close the service by urging those who were interested in committing their lives to Christ to retire to a nearby room where the deacons would counsel with them.[17] Almost every Sunday many would retire to the designated room to commit their lives to Christ.

How to Give the Invitation

There is no sure-fire plan. One cannot write out a formula for the public invitation. Congregations are as different in personality and temperament as are individuals. No wise preacher will superimpose a system upon his audience. He will guard against violating personality. It is only possible to offer some suggestions which will contain a few fundamental principles.

1. The preacher must bring himself to the proper frame of mind. It must begin in the heart of the evangelist. He must be gravely concerned for the lost in the audience. He must come to this concern and poise through much prayer. He should begin

praying for the invitation period the day before it is given. Let him pray until his greatest desire is to see the lost saved. Paul said, "Knowing therefore the terror of the Lord, we persuade men" (II Cor. 5:11). Lost men are under the wrath of God (John 3:36). They are not aware of their condition. The evangelist knows this and must, by his firm, tender pleas, lead the sinner to realize his guilt before God. Mere perfunctory concern in the evangelist cannot be used of God to bring a sense of dire need in the sinner's heart. The proper attitude of the evangelist is a gift of the Holy Spirit.

2. Plan the invitation. The invitation must be as carefully planned as the body of the sermon. The Holy Spirit can use a well-planned sermon far more effectively than a poorly prepared one. The same thing is true with the climax of the sermon. Plan the invitation and then remain alert to the Spirit and follow Him in the use of the plan. Be prepared to alter or completely omit any part of the planned invitation. Do your best in organization and offer it to the Holy Spirit. He may see fit to brush aside the entire plan. The preacher is prepared only when he is prepared to follow without reserve every prompting of the Holy Spirit.

3. Give the invitation with poise. Dr. C. E. Matthews was possibly the most effective evangelist at this point that Southern Baptists ever knew. When he walked upon the platform to preach and invite men to God in a great Sunday morning revival hour, he was the essence of poise. It was not the air of being cocksure, but it was a humble confidence in God. He knew how, and he knew God would give him the ability to perform. He was not timid. He was as bold as a lion and as humble as a lamb at the same time. Dr. Matthews, Dr. Scarborough, Dr. Carroll, and in fact all effective soul-winners, never said, "Is there one who will accept Christ today?" They would say, "How many will now accept the Saviour?"

The preacher with poise will expect great things to happen every time he preaches Christ. His confidence in the Gospel will give him poise. The effective evangelist will avoid extreme physical gestures in the pulpit. It is not necessary and it is fleshly to cry out in the beginning of the invitation, "Come on! Come on!" etc. This is the time to be tender, sweet, persuasive, yet firm. Don't move men with blood-curdling shouts in the invitation, but let the Holy Spirit move them with His still, small voice.

4. Give the invitation clearly. Make the plan of salvation plain. Make each proposition plain. Speak the language of the audience. When men understand clearly what is said, only then can the truth be effective. Christ spoke plainly, using a language easily understood by all, and the multitudes heard Him gladly. Do not mix the propositions. While men are urged to confess Christ as Saviour, be sure to make it clear if they are asked also to unite with the church. Men must know what they are doing. Often the invitation to accept Christ is an invitation to ask for church membership. If this is the purpose of the proposition, be sure to make it clear. If the preacher fails to make clear his proposition, confusion will prevail to the hurt of all concerned. In a rural church in Louisiana on one occasion, an invitation was given with too little clarity. When an Intermediate girl came forward, the preacher asked, "How do you come tonight?" She naturally answered, "I came in the wagon with my grandmother." It is so easy for an audience to misunderstand even a clear proposition, much less one fraught with ambiguity.

Several propositions may be given at the same time if each one is clearly presented. The evangelist might begin by stating, "The following should respond: First, those who are Christians but have never followed Christ in baptism. These should come now and follow Christ all the way. Secondly, all who are not Christians, but realizing that you are lost, that you need a Saviour, that Christ is the Saviour, but that He cannot save you unless you are willing — will you come forward, and express a willingness to receive Him?" The evangelist can give several propositions at the same time without mixing them to the point of confusion.

5. Give the invitation courteously.[18] The soul-winner must respect the rights of others, even the right to die in their sins if they persist. It never pays to embarrass others. A preacher should be as courteous in the sacred pulpit as he is in the home of his host. To trick people into a position of embarrassment is discourteous. Let the audience know that it can trust you, and then you can lead them to trust your Christ. Be a gentleman at all times. A gentleman will refrain from taking advantage of anyone at any time. One may reply, "The devil has taken advantage of

them to send them to hell, why not use every means to bring them to God?" The retort may sound acceptable until you examine it. The sinner will never be led to see your honest, fair, gentle, saving Christ through your breastworks of dishonest, unfair, ungentlemanly acts. The greatest evangelists have been courteous men. They have never found it necessary to resort to instruments of the flesh to further God's cause.

6. Depend at all times on the Holy Spirit. The Holy Spirit is more concerned about the results of any given service than any Christian could ever be. He will be present, and He will guide if permitted to do so. When He is present and when He is given complete charge, whatever transpires will be correct and proper. We can trust the Holy Spirit. He ripens the grain. He prepares for the harvest.

7. Extend the invitation the proper length of time. Do not stop too soon. Let the invitation run as long as folk are moving and the Spirit is working. The congregation will not resent a long service if God is working in the hearts of neighbors. It is tragic, however, to extend the invitation unduly. The leaders of the service should be able to discern when the time to conclude has arrived.

Types of Invitation

1. There are two types of invitation: the invitation to the Christians, and the invitation to the unsaved. Christians should not be ignored in our public invitations. Revival almost always begins with the Christian and not with the unsaved.[19] After a sermon on "Sins That Hinder God's People" or a kindred subject, the evangelist may urge the Christians to lift their hands in confession of their sins or to come forward rededicating themselves to God. He may preach on the "Home" or the "Need for Prayer" and then call on the people to come forward and dedicate their homes to God, pledging by so doing to set up family altars. He may explain how one may institute a family altar. Often people are hungry to do a particular thing but are frightened away from it by not knowing how to begin. Let the evangelist tell them that they may begin a family altar by calling the family together once each day. Let the father or mother read a brief passage from the Bible; then every member of the family bow and pray silently. Soon the day will come when they will all be able to pray brief audible prayers after the Holy Word has

been read. When the plan has been explained, let the choir sing while whole families come down front signifying their willingness to try the home prayer altar. At the close of the invitation, let the pastor pray a prayer of dedication. When prayer fires burn in the homes, revival fires will burn in the church.

Call Christians to a deeper spiritual life. Often God's people become lukewarm and lose their concern for the lost. They need to be shocked into realizing the sin of unconcern. A sermon on the "Obligations of the Redeemed" will awaken them from this spiritual lethargy. It is not enough to awaken them. They must be put into action for God or they will turn over and go back to sleep. This may be done by calling upon them to seal the resolve, which is now in their hearts, by a public stand, thereby surrendering to God for a more faithful attendance at worship and a pledge to win souls.

2. The second type of invitation is to the unsaved. First, the regular invitation. Usually the unsaved person is asked to do certain definite things, such as to hold up the hand if concerned to the extent he wishes the Christian to pray for him. After prayer, he is asked to confess in his heart that he is a sinner and needs salvation. Then he is asked to call on Christ for soul salvation. Finally, he is urged to come forward, thus publicly confessing Christ. When he comes to the front, the preacher at the altar speaks briefly with him and beckons him to be seated. If it is clear that he understands the plan of salvation, his name is presented to the church as a candidate for church membership. He is received as a candidate — he is not a member of the church and will not be until he has been properly instructed and baptized. This is the method commonly used in the southern part of the United States where the invitation is as old as the civilization.

The invitation may be varied.

(1) There is the progressive invitation.[20] In this type of invitation, progressive steps are used to get the people to completely surrender to Christ. While the congregation is still seated, the evangelist asks the convicted to raise their hands for prayer. Those who lifted their hands are asked to stand while the evangelist prays for them. After the prayer, the entire congregation stands, and those who were prayed for are urged to come forward. This method should not be used except by seasoned

preachers who know how to shun high pressure. It should not be used by them unless the spiritual atmosphere is right. Too often, this method has been abused.

(2) Another variation is the testimony invitation.[21] After the sermon and after the first appeal, the evangelist will have some highly respected Christian, regardless of age, give a brief three- or four-minute testimony, telling how he was converted. Then the invitation is continued. As long as the response is fair, continue the invitation. When the response ebbs, another exemplary Christian, who has been alerted in advance to be ready, is called forward to give his testimony. These testimonies will warm the hearts and encourage the people who are under conviction. Often these testimonies will solve the particular difficulty which the sinner in the audience is at grips with. New converts with their testimony will often stir the audience more deeply than anyone else. Each testimony is followed with singing. This type of invitation is better suited to youth-led revivals but may be used any time in any audience.

(3) It is often effective to have the audience remain seated and bow for prayer while the evangelist makes clear the proposition. The people who should respond are given a chance to get up from their seats and quietly come forward. This kind of invitation is most effective in large audiences. There should be no singing, only soft organ or piano music.

(4) The majority of experienced evangelists and pastors are generally inclined to close the sermon with a heart appeal, and have the audience stand and join the choir in singing some familiar invitation song while the convicted are given a chance to move forward. As long as the response is good, nothing is said, only the voices of the singing. When the response dies down, the evangelist makes brief appeals between verses to answer certain problems which tend to hold back the convicted. This type of appeal is the most popular and is freer from tricks and high pressure.

(5) The inquiry room. Often in union meetings or city-wide campaigns, the person under conviction is urged to come to the front as an indication of his concern. After the invitation, those responding are ushered to another room or to an adjacent tent, and trained personal workers deal with each one individually. After the personal work by soul-winners, the evangelist

generally gives instructions to the group. He will explain again the plan of salvation. He usually tells them to read their Bible daily, pray, give their testimony, and attend the church of their choice the very next Lord's Day to take a public stand for Christ in the local church. As we have seen, this type of invitation comes down to us in a modified form from Asahel Nettleton, Dwight L. Moody, Spurgeon, and others.

WHO GIVES THE INVITATION

The evangelist does not give the invitation alone. If he does, it is sure to end in failure. One of our greatest evangelists points out that many are involved in the invitation.[22] The evangelist, choir, congregation, pastor, and the Holy Spirit are all involved in the invitation.

1. The evangelist has an unescapable responsibility. The evangelist will use every power available to him. He will use the power of persuasion, psychology, and organization.[23] He will talk during the invitation only when necessary. He will use every argument fitting that given congregation in the course of the invitation, if necessity dictates. Those in the audience who stand under conviction of their need but hesitate to make the decision, will be addressed earnestly by the preacher. Those who are afraid they could not quit drinking or cursing will be helped in the course of the invitation. How does the evangelist know which difficulties to deal with? If he is an efficient evangelist, he will visit and talk with people daily. He will see these folk with difficulties seated in his audience. He knows that these difficulties, which he has faced each day in the field, probably represent the difficulties of many to whom he has not spoken personally.

The battle of a soul is usually fought around one sin, not a flock of sins. If a person can win the victory over that one besetting sin, he can battle the others too. Each sinner has a darling sin, just one. He is guilty of several, but only one is his darling sin. Make him face it. Tell him that he is free to go on enjoying the thrill of that sin, but if he does he must pay the price. The price is death. The price is too much to pay for the value received. Use illustrations to make plain his folly and the wages of sin. Urge him to make Christ, the Prince of Peace, his Lord and desert the tyrant who now rules him with an iron fist and promises nought but endless night in return. Persuade men.

All who remember the "terror of the Lord" and the "love of Christ" will persuade with power.

2. The pastor's place. The evangelist works on a team in the public invitation. The church loves the pastor and the sight of him at the altar marshals their prayer and concern. The pastor prays silently as he stands quietly at the altar. He does not lift his hand or exhort. If he does, the point of focus is split. Only one man can direct the invitation. Either the evangelist who is conducting the meeting or the pastor should direct the invitation. The logical one is the evangelist. The pastor may feel free to take over and direct the invitation at any time and the evangelist will welcome it, but the pastor should not stand down front and attract attention by lifting his hands or speaking while the evangelist is in charge. The pastor will warmly shake hands with those coming forward and speak to them briefly. If large numbers are coming forward, it would be better if he only grips their hand and seats them. Then when the response has abated and while the evangelist pleads, the pastor may sit or kneel by the converts and talk personally with each. The response often comes in waves. If the pastor talks unduly long with one person and people are waiting in the aisles, the wave may be broken. Maybe it should be stopped, but remember the minutes of the invitation are precious. The atmosphere is delicate, and the least thing may completely interfere.

The pastor will always conclude the invitation. He may not feel led to exhort or continue the decision periods, but the way he conducts himself in recognizing those who came forward will greatly affect the whole atmosphere of the service and prepare the way for the next decision period. If he gives due consideration to everyone who comes forward and is fair to all, those in the congregation who needed to respond but for various reasons or excuses did not, will feel drawn to him.

3. The choir is next in importance to the pastor and the evangelist in extending the invitation. The Gospel in song is vital. Music appears to be just as effective as the sermon in bringing the Gospel and in some instances even more so. The choir has a grave responsibility in inviting the lost to the Saviour. If the music director and choir know what the preacher expects, they will co-operate with him. He should talk with them before the service about the song for the invitation and how he wants

it done. The choir should pray before every service. Every member of the choir should be as consecrated as the preacher. When the preacher comes to the invitation, the sign should be given the song leader, and the organist will sound the chord as the choir rises to its feet. It will rise singing the first stanza. They will lead the congregation. The congregation may sing without the use of a book in the invitation. The choir will sing one verse after another without a pause until the preacher indicates a break. They will sing the same invitation song until the preacher indicates a change.

The majority of preachers will trust the song leader to plan all the music for the service. He should have this responsibility unless he has no conception of a revival service. This would certainly be an exception, for our seminaries are training our music men properly. The preacher should select the invitation song. He knows in advance what proposition he plans to present and which song will best suit the invitation.

4. Many church members are not aware that they have an obligation in the invitation. Often they fold their arms or reach for their coats and begin thinking about something else. Little do they realize that they are almost as responsible for the lost in the congregation and the results of that service as the preacher. This is tragic and should be changed. It can be changed. The pastor must inform the people as to their responsibility as well as privilege. The congregation should co-operate in three ways:

(1) They may sing. They should sing without books. A young preacher in one of my classes at the seminary told me that he learned to sing tenor hiding behind a songbook to keep from confessing Christ as Saviour. The least thing will serve as a prop to hold back a sinner under conviction.

(2) The congregation should pray. Often the preacher will feel the Spirit of God during the sermon, but when the invitation begins, the service seems to freeze over. Why? Often it is due to the indifference of the congregation. But the power of God works mightily in a congregation really praying. Instruct the Christians to beam their prayers on some lost person in the congregation. This instruction must, of course, not be given in an open gospel service. It will be given in advance during a session of preparation.

(3) The congregation may do personal work. They will be

cautious at this juncture. The unchurched do not as a rule resent being spoken to in public if it is done without attracting attention. If the personal worker is seated beside or near the prospect and quietly approaches him, he will be effective. Personal workers, Sunday School teachers, and staff members of the church should be trained and organized for personal work in the audience.

5. We have already referred to the vital place of the Holy Spirit in the invitation. Results received without His help will be worse than useless.

(1) All involved will rely on the Holy Spirit for guidance and power. Two things guarantee a successful evangelistic service; namely, prospects in earnest and power of the Holy Spirit. The house may be filled with prospects, but if there is no power in the service, they will go away unmoved. The Holy Spirit brings the power. The whole place may be electrified with spiritual power, yet there can be no visible results unless the unsaved are present.

(2) Give Him a chance to work. God is a jealous God and will not share His glory with any man. All human instruments must get out of the way or be completely surrendered as tools in God's hands.

(3) Give Him credit. One's conduct and work after a great and fruitful service will prepare for the very next battle. If one is so blind and self-centered as to intimate his part in the previous victory, he, by so doing, disqualifies himself for the next step in the success of the revival. When the flesh enters, God departs. Fleshliness is the devil hard at work. He thus kills many revivals.

CHAPTER 10

CONSERVATION OF RESULTS

When one is confronted with the Gospel and led to accept Jesus Christ as his Saviour, by faith his soul is saved. However, that is only the initial stage in the Christian life. The life must be saved also. To do this, every noble resolve must be channeled; every lofty experience must be capitalized on; and every power set in motion by the experience must be harnessed. True evangelism is not merely concerned with an experience of soul salvation, but it is interested in keeping the convert in proper relation to God and leading him into rich Christian living. Evangelism which stops with conversion is incomplete and has not accomplished its full, intended purpose. Conservation is given major emphasis all through the Bible. As long as evangelism has been clearly defined in the mind of God's people, God has laid a strong emphasis on consolidation. "Spare not, lengthen thy cords, and strengthen thy stakes" (Isa. 54:2). Here the emphases are twofold: Enlarge the place of the tent; and consolidate the results. The same note was sounded by the Son of God centuries later when Jesus commanded His followers to "Go ye therefore, and disciple all nations . . . teaching them" (Matt. 28:19-20).[1] In the Old Testament God had commanded them to "lengthen thy cords," and Jesus tells them to what extent, "disciple all nations." In Isaiah God told His people to "strengthen thy stakes," and Jesus explained, "teaching them to observe all things whatsoever I have commanded you." It is not enough to bring new converts into the fold; they must be developed. They must have knowledge of what God expects of them and how to perform in the battle of life. This is conservation.

THE NEED FOR CONSERVATION

1. Prevailing conditions in the majority of our evangelical churches testify to the need for a vigorous program of conserva-

tion. It is common knowledge that almost ninety-five per cent of our members never win anyone outside the church to Christ. This is a tragedy and it is not the fault of the average church member. The failure lies in the church. It has failed to teach and direct the new convert to the main task of every believer. It has taken for granted that all converts will go out and win others. All have had the urge, but only a few ever follow through without direction and encouragement from the church. In most cases, the church has given neither.

About fifty per cent of our church members do not attend Sunday School, and another sixty per cent never attend the evening preaching service. Seventy per cent never give to missions and leave the burden of world missions on the shoulders of only thirty per cent of the fold. We can readily see from these figures that evangelism suffers at home and abroad when a thorough program of conservation is neglected. Incomplete evangelism is the most expensive failure of the church.

Twenty-four per cent of our members are detached.[2] They have moved to another community and have not united with a church where they live. They are lost to the church. There are enough detached members among Southern Baptists alone to constitute nine thousand average-size churches, or twenty-four hundred churches of one thousand members, or forty-eight hundred churches with a membership of five hundred each. If these detached members were enlisted and gave in proportion to those who are enlisted, their gifts each year would amount to eighteen million dollars for missions and sixty million dollars for local activity. If they won souls to Christ in proportion to those now enlisted, they would win one hundred thousand to Christ annually. There is also another twenty-five per cent living within the area of the church who are unenlisted and just as lost to us. It is believed that the condition of Southern Baptists at this point is general among the evangelicals of our land. This is a dreadful price to pay for an inadequate program of conservation.

Do not let the local church excuse itself from failure to measure up to this responsibility. There is no reason for such weakness. These delinquent members are not hypocrites, nor may we label them as unconverted souls. They are delinquent children of a preoccupied mother. Just as a newborn babe depends upon his parents for care, food, shelter, and education, so is the new convert dependent upon the church for spiritual food, loving care, and edification.

2. The need for a solid work of conservation is seen in the nature of the new convert. Some think of the convert as a person who has received a great work of grace and from now on should live an upright life because of this work of grace. They think he should be able to stand on his own feet. The truth is that the new Christian is a babe in Christ and must learn how to walk, talk, and combat effectively the forces of evil. It is the obligation of the church to teach him how to walk. His legs will at first be unsteady and his knees weak. He will wobble and fall a few times, but he is a healthy baby learning to walk. The mother must ever keep her eye on him, and her hands under his arms until he has learned to walk upright. The same skilful patience is needed in every other phase of the child's development. The gravest hour in the life of a home is when a little child has been born into it. There will be many more grave and momentous hours to come later. The most serious obligation of all comes to a church when a lost soul is saved and united with it. Its obligation does not end, but really begins when a convert enters its fold. It takes just as much genuine interest and concern after the convert is added to the church rolls as while he was being brought to Christ. Men are not saved merely to go to heaven when they die. They are saved to serve. The new convert must be informed of his obligation to serve and he must receive instruction as to how he can serve.

SOME ESSENTIALS IN CONSERVATION

1. It is necessary that every convert unite with a local church. Evangelism must always add to the local church. Every new Christian should be led to unite with a church of his choice. To win one to Christ and fail to lead him into a local church is to deny him every blessing and privilege that that divine institution has to offer. It is to depart from the evangelism of Christ and Paul. Paul's program of conservation included the church. He organized churches in each community and went back often to instruct the group. The early believers believed that they should continue "stedfastly in the apostles' doctrine and fellowship, and in breaking of bread, and in prayers" (Acts 2:42).

2. Sound preaching and trustworthy methods must be employed by the evangelist and pastor. Conservation begins with

the preacher. The purpose of the evangelist must be correct. His prime purpose will not be numbers. He will lead the church to win all reasonably possible to Christ, but not by high pressure. The future of the local church and the future of the individual believer will be prominent in the thinking of the evangelist. He will therefore refrain from tricks and traps in his invitations. It will be well to be sure of the preaching methods of the evangelist you wish to employ. This writer has seen people brought into the membership of local churches under conditions which would make impossible any program of consolidation. All evangelism methods should magnify the glory of God.

3.   Proper organization is essential.

(1)   Provide adequate space. Someone has said "a healthy turtle will grow a shell large enough in which to live." This may be true of turtles, but the shell of a church can become formless and unrelated unless it is planned wisely. The building should be well planned and made ready for the growth of the expanding church and all of its organizations.

The average church has auditorium space sufficient for only about one-half of the local membership. We must expect their presence at worship and provide for it.

(2)   Adequate leadership must be provided. Every church could have many more in attendance in its Bible school and training units if it had enough trained leaders. There is not one church in forty which has provided enough leadership to meet the local needs.

4.   A thorough follow-up is essential.

(1)   Let the pastor have the new convert in his office immediately for a personal conference. The pastor will do three things in this conference. First, he will make sure that the individual is truly converted. Secondly, he will make clear the relation of the pastor to the convert. He will assure him that he desires to help him in every way, and that he stands ready at all times to serve him as pastor. Thirdly, he will tell him about the pastor's class which meets every Sunday night during the Training Union hour. The convert will study for six Sunday nights under the pastor's leadership. The pastor will teach him the meaning of salvation. He will tell him about the benefits of the church, his relation to the church, and its relation to the denomination and the entire Christian world. He will be in-

structed in the doctrines of the faith. He will be graduated from
the pastor's class into the training organization where he will be
trained in church membership.

(2) The Training Union should visit the new member of
the church before the following Sunday. He will be introduced
to the leaders of the particular union which he will be expected
to attend. These same leaders will come for him on the last
night of the pastor's class and induct him into the union.

(3) The Sunday School, Brotherhood, and WMU will all
properly contact and enlist the new member.

(4) The deacons will visit him before the following Sunday to acquaint him with the system of finance and give him
necessary instructions. He will be asked to pledge to the financial
support of the church. The time to enlist a member in the total
life of the church is promptly after his induction.

5. The church must be spiritual. A warm spirit is essential
to the well-being of its members.

(1) Hot servings of the whole Gospel must constantly flow
from the pulpit. The souls of men are hungry. Men long for and
need the milk and meat of the Word. If a given restaurant
serves nourishing meals and does it well, soon the entire community will know it and crowd in for service. The same thing is
true of the church with a pulpit in constant touch with the
heavenly bakery.

(2) Divine currents of power must permeate the church.[3]
Only then can the church draw people and nurture them. These
currents are not emotional but spiritual. They are not trumped
up by the energy of the flesh; they are currents of spiritual power
from the throbbing presence of the living God. This spiritual
power will be recognized by all present. The convert will not be
able to explain it, but because of it he will know that something
is there which is bigger than himself and which could only
come from Almighty God. This divine power will have an inte-
grating effect. The writer was once employed digging ditches
and laying pipes for the purpose of moving natural gas from one
section of the country to another. We found that in certain areas
there were chemicals in the soil, which quickly disintegrated the
steel pipes. This was remedied by charging the pipe-line with
electricity. Not only did the electricity prevent corrosion, but it
actually transformed the particles of rust into steel again and

integrated them into the pipe. This is exactly what happens in a healthy church as new members are being integrated into the life of the local church. If the church doesn't have this divine current working through it, all else in conservation will be futile.

(3) The church must promote world vision. The church which cannot see beyond its own little bailiwick will soon see little of its bailiwick. When we feed our members on a vision of world need, we grow mighty men of tall stature. No man is likely to hear the cry of a needy soul at his door unless he can see the beckoning hand from afar. He may be deaf and blind to both unless his church enlightens him.

How to Organize for Conservation

1. Magnify the reception of the new member.

(1) Take time to properly receive him when he presents himself for membership. We are often in too great haste at the conclusion of the service. Some pastors say a special word of commendation and praise, and then have members of the family or Sunday School teachers come forward to stand by the new recruit while he is being fellowshiped.

(2) Train the whole church to come by and give the convert a warm hand of welcome.

(3) Give the new joiner a Bible when he unites with the church.

(4) Let the church give a special social for him soon after his reception. At this social have the officers of the various organizations present to meet and fellowship the newly inducted member. We get acquainted more readily with new people when we play, laugh, and worship with them. Some churches do not receive applicants for church membership when they present themselves in an open worship service. They are required to come before a committee and the pastor, and sometimes they are placed in special training classes before they are accepted into the church. This prevails especially on foreign fields. Where this is the practice, the manner of magnifying his reception will be altered to suit the situation. In any case, the importance of the decision should be given proper emphasis, and warm cordial care must be given the young Christian. The examining and preparations committee will not sit as cold judges but will operate as friendly, cordial helpers. Members of the committee

will be mindful of the timidity of the new convert. Relatives and friends will be invited to attend the committee or board meeting with him. A spirit of prayer and understanding must permeate such meetings.

2. Provide the new member with a packet of certain informative material. The material should consist of a tract informing him about the church. It should contain also a copy of the church covenant, a pledge card, a copy of the state paper, and a card to be filled out, checking the type of service he would prefer to perform in the church.

3. Assign each new member to a seasoned Christian for at least three months. The new convert is a babe in Christ and may act like one unless he is guarded and helped by the more mature members of the church. Recently a man was converted out of a vile background and united with the church. Less than a week from the time of his public profession of faith, he was seen at a public gathering with the smell of beer on his breath. In view of his background this was no reflection on his conversion, but if he had been found drinking beer three months later it would be a reflection on both his conversion and his church. It would be the duty of the seasoned Christian, in whose care the new member is placed, to instruct and guide him in such matters. The seasoned Christian will visit his new responsibility once a week and teach him to read the Bible daily, to pray each day, to attend prayer meeting, and church twice on Sunday. He will also teach him the art of soul-winning. He will report once each month to the pastor or the committee on conservation.

4. Give the new member a suitable place of service. If we do not use him, we may lose him. No one should idly warm a bench for long. Who are the faithful members of your church? They are the people with definite tasks to perform. It is a known fact that people often leave a large church to serve in a smaller, less effective one. The devout Christian had rather serve his God in a small, weak church with perhaps a less powerful preacher and limited equipment, than to be idle in the best church on earth. Men are not only held by a task, but they are developed and made strong by exercising their talents. The idle Christian is easy prey for Satan. There is a job for every Christian. It doesn't matter how large or small the church, the wide-awake church will find a place of activity for every Christian.

5. Send birthday and anniversary cards to every member. Many pastors take time to carry a birthday card to every member each year. The task of conservation does not end with the first three or four months of concerted effort. The church is responsible for each member until his death. The church must constantly work at conservation. It is a process which is endless. Many a Christian is backslidden and idle today who was once active and thoroughly enlisted. There is no place or time to let up in conservation.

6. Write letters.[4] Send a letter on each anniversary of baptism. Write a few letters every day to some of the members. Write to the faithful and commend them. They will love you for it and never forget it. Write those in trouble or discouraged. Write those away from home on business or vacation. Write young people in college and let them know you are counting on them. Urge them to unite with a church where they live. Write them when they have done something special, such as graduating from high school or college. Write them if they receive promotions or do something outstanding. Let them know you are interested enough to stay informed about them.

7. Enlist them in the total ministry of the church.

(1) Use the new member in soul-winning. He knows very little about it, but he is willing. If left unsought a few months he may have lost the willingness. Teach him the art of soul-winning.

(2) Enlist him in Bible study. This is the purpose of the Sunday School.

(3) Train him through the Training Union to be an effective church member.

(4) Lead him in scriptural giving.

(5) Bring him into the worship services of the church.

The average church will be tempted to take short cuts in this program, but Dr. Sweazey points out that short cuts in evangelism may be disastrous.[5] The most expensive cut any church ever made was a short cut in evangelism. Short cuts in conservation are costing Southern Baptists alone today over two hundred thousand converts and $156,000,000 annually. Churches which recognize this and do a consistently good job annually in conservation are showing far greater growth than those that take short cuts. Any church which cares to do a thorough job in conservation could double its membership every year. The reason is clear because, as it enlists and trains its members, it will increase the number of soul-winners and the capacity to conserve. The fear that a church might take in more members than it can assimilate is unfounded. They often do, but such is unexcusable. If good methods for assimilating new members are used, the church need never fear that it is receiving too many new members. The good methods must be *used*, however. To have the blueprints or even the machinery is absolutely not enough. Someone must be responsible to press the button and throw the machinery into motion. Nothing will work of itself. It must be worked.

Chapter 11

RURAL EVANGELISM

Rural churches differ from each other widely as to background, nature, and outlook. Rural communities are made up of all types of people. Some of the rural people have been farmers for generations, while others are former factory workers and some of them are now living in semi-commercial areas. Some are migrants, merchants, school teachers, workers in salt mills, laborers in the woods of logging concerns, and many other types. Some rural folk live in towns of twenty-five hundred or less, while others live far out in sparsely settled regions. Rural people are possibly more difficult to classify than the people who live in the cities. There is a larger variety of personality to be found in the rural area than anywhere else.

The rural church may be defined as a church in the open country or in towns of twenty-five hundred or less. A few rural churches are well organized and are trained sufficiently to provide a high order of worship and accomplishment, while others are poorly trained and poorly organized. Due to lack of training many of them are inadequate for the challenge of the present complex hour.

The Challenge of Rural Evangelism

Basically, evangelism for the rural areas should not differ from evangelism in large towns and cities. There will be slight variations as to the methods to be used to meet the local needs. It may often be necessary to vary the evangelistic methods but never the evangelistic emphasis.[1] But this emphasis in the country should be as firm and as well promoted as in the urban sections.

1. Enlistment is one of the crucial problems of rural churches.[2] To enlist the church members who are resident but inactive and lead them to attend the regular services of the

church is a difficult problem; it is pre-evangelism. To lead those who attend church regularly but who are not active in soul-winning is just another step in meeting the same problem. This is as true of the city churches as it is of the rural churches. Throughout the Southern Baptist Convention only fifty-one per cent of the total membership is enlisted. Twenty-five per cent of the total membership is unaffiliated, and another twenty-four per cent lives in the community but is not active.[3] This leakage will neutralize our efforts in evangelism if it is not curbed. 76.4 per cent of Southern Baptist churches are in the open country, village, and town.[4] This means that 22,920 of Southern Baptists' 30,000 churches are rural or semi-rural. 48.4 per cent of the total number of Southern Baptist churches are actually in the open country. If the leakage in the rural churches is in proportion to the waste in the city churches, then the major challenge of enlistment stems from both the rural and town churches. Since this waste tends to neutralize the effects of evangelism, it becomes one of the basic problems of rural evangelism.

2. The opportunity for soul-winning is tremendous. In 1900 only thirty-six per cent of the total population of the United States were church members. By 1940, forty-nine per cent were members of the churches and in 1953 the number had climbed to fifty-nine per cent.[5] In 1956, sixty per cent of the population of the nation had religious affiliation.[6] We are primarily concerned with the location of the unchurched of our nation. Ordinarily one would think that the vast majority of them are in the cities, and it is true that the majority of them are there. But Dr. Schnucker points out that in 1953, an amazing percentage of the unchurched of the nation were in the towns and open country.[7] In 1956, 61,796,897 of the total population of the nation was located in the open country and towns.[8] In 1953 a survey revealed that seventy-four per cent of the rural people in the Pacific Northwest were unchurched. In the Midwest in 1952 a survey in a semi-rural area was made, showing that ninety-two per cent of the inhabitants of a small city of five thousand held church membership, while in the same rural area in the same county only sixty-six per cent of the rural population held church membership.[9]

In 1935, seventy per cent of the Southern Baptist population was rural.[10] In 1956 slightly less than fifty per cent of Southern

Baptist membership was in rural churches. This points to two facts: first, that Southern Baptists are concentrating their evangelistic efforts in the urban areas; and second, that the population in rural areas is possibly becoming less and less. Groups like Southern Baptists can be happy for their gains in the cities, but they should be disturbed about the sagging of evangelism in the country. In 1956 Southern Baptists' town and open-country churches baptized 165,334, while urban churches which constitute only 23.6 per cent of the total number of churches, baptized 217,802.[11]

Sixty-seven million of our population are without any religious affiliation.[12] It is estimated that 30,162,586 of this number reside in the rural areas.[13] This means that better than one-third of the total unchurched population of the nation resides in rural territory. The records of the Home Mission Council reveal that ten thousand village and rural areas in America are without a church of any kind, Jewish, Roman Catholic, or Protestant, and that thirty thousand villages are without a pastor.[14]

3. The ratio of baptisms in rural churches is below that of urban churches. In 1956 the ratio of baptisms in the open-country church was one to every 27.3 members. In the cities the same year the ratio was one to every 20.7. The town churches did better than the churches in the open country according to this same record. The town churches were able to baptize one for every twenty-three members.[15] These figures in themselves emphasize the need for rural evangelism.

4. Migrant laborers, tenant farmers, and small groups of public workers isolated in rural communities should be met with the Gospel. At harvest time, in many sections of rural America, great crowds of migrant laborers come to the fields for employment. The migrant workers in the wheat belt of the Middle West, in the fruit and vegetable region of the Pacific Coast, the cranberry acreage of New York, and the beet fields of Colorado constitute the major challenge at this point. The migrant is generally looked upon as unstable in character and a necessary nuisance. Many of them, however, are fine people, and all of them need spiritual guidance and love. The migrant should be reached by the rural church.

Special meetings with both social and spiritual care should be given. The church may use its basement for reading room, games, and singing. The men may be urged to write there to their loved ones at home. Brief, lively services may be held for them. Tracts and Bibles should be given out, and well-trained men should do direct soul-winning. Often those whom we consider worthless are stimulated by our making them feel wanted and important. Many will respond to kindness and a brotherly attitude. No one wants to be looked down upon, and most persons will respond to a wholesome spirit of real unselfishness. When the social and religious atmosphere of the harvest area is friendly, the tired soul of the migrant is usually responsive. It has been proved in many areas that the migrants will go to the Sunday services in reasonably large numbers if the atmosphere is friendly and inviting, rather than cold and standoffish.

The tenant farmer should be a recipient of the blessings of rural evangelism rather than its problem. A survey was made several years ago in seventy counties in the South which revealed that white tenant farmers comprise 38.5 per cent of the total farm-operating group while 26.5 per cent were farm owners. The survey showed that the churches were satisfactorily reaching the farm-owner group, but for some reason they were doing poorly among the tenants. It was also revealed that if the churches in the seventy counties were reaching the tenants and the farm owners in the same ratio, more than ten thousand more members would be enrolled in the churches of the seventy-county area.[16] Many of the unchurched people in the rural areas are tenants. A vigorous and attractive program of evangelism is needed at this point. As a rule the tenant farmer is transient, but this constitutes a challenge rather than a problem. Most of the tenants are uneducated, and this factor must be kept in mind as these folk are evangelized. Their background is in many ways different from the background of the factory worker in the crowded cities. Tenants have a better knowledge of the Bible, and they adhere to a higher personal standard for the most part, yet they are not any easier to reach with evangelism. They are more individualistic and move more slowly toward any organized effort or becoming a member of something. The tenant problem, like all other problems in the country, is not uniform. Statistics find no parallels in rural America. Percentages are not the same across the country. In some counties over fifty per cent of the church membership is made up of tenants; in others, less than twenty-five per cent. In a few communities, tenant farmers serve as leaders in the churches, while in others almost none of the leaders are tenants. An aggressive program of rural evangelism can change that picture. Membership and leadership should almost always be in proportion to the size of each group in their particular area. The Lord has no respect of persons. He loves all and wants to save and use all. An attractive program of evangelism will take no account of persons except to shape its approach to win and enlist them for Christ.

5. The youth population in the rural areas constitutes one of the greatest challenges to evangelism. It has been discovered that almost half of America's children are still within reach of town and open-country churches. Our conclusion is drawn from the fact that of the 1,502,710 children in America over five years old, forty per cent of them are in areas within reach of the rural and open-country church.[17] These young people could and should be reached by a well-planned and vigorous Sunday School effort. To reach them we need especially more and larger Sunday Schools with better buildings.

HINDRANCES TO RURAL EVANGELISM

1. Changes are not as readily accepted in the country as they are in the cities. This fact, as one may well see, is one of the serious hindrances to rural evangelism. There was a time when rural people were very slow to accept and use modern methods.[18] This condition has passed completely in a few areas and is slowly giving way generally. This is due to the new improvements in agricultural methods and equipment, new rural schools, better roads, cars, television, etc. There are still too many communities where changes for better living have been adopted by the community, but the old church which their fathers built is still using the same evangelistic techniques employed many years ago. Dr. Jent said, "A 'pioneer' church in the midst of modern life is a 'misfit.'"[19] Sentiment and tradition still remain in the open country to stunt evangelism and religious progress. Preaching, singing, and praying can no longer make up all of the religious program of the rural church. There was a time when it was sufficient, but rural life is becoming increasingly complex. We are to do no less preaching, singing, and praying, but there must be added a teaching program. The social life must be min-

istered to by the church. The rural church in this day must be organized.[20] It must train its youth, direct the activity of its men, and utilize the energy of its women. If it provides organization for its youth, men, and women, it will need to build larger and different styled buildings. It should provide an educational building as well as an ample auditorium. It is the task of the church to preserve the naturalness, beauty, and simplicity of rural life, but at the same time promote and stimulate moral, religious, and social progress.[21]

When a community dies, the cause can almost always be traced back to the local church. If the church is progressive and engenders a spirit of righteousness, good will, and co-operation, the community will usually prosper. If the church stagnates, before long the community may follow and virtually disintegrate. Why should a community die? The soil is there; the brooks, hills, and plains are constant. Then why should a community die? The people themselves make the difference. Stagnation has often been bred in the community by negative approach and appeal. Often the appeal is gloomy and too little has been said or done to encourage fellowship and co-operation. At this very juncture, a bright, attractive, and optimistic program of evangelism can be of untold value to the whole life of the community.

2. Rural churches are often hindered by inadequate organization. The membership is not sufficiently trained. They have not been taught to give. They do not have enough money to prosecute an attractive program of evangelism. If they witness a splendid ingathering from a special revival, they do not have the money to conserve the results nor the necessary leadership to form an organization sufficient to sustain the evangelistic program. It is imperative, therefore, that the church grow a healthy organization and build an adequate building if it is to promote an adequate program of evangelism.

3. The leadership is often inadequate.[22] When the leadership is strong, intelligent, and progressive, the churches grow and are well attended. It matters not where the church is located; with God's help it will grow if it has capable, alert, and consecrated leadership. When the leaders lead, the rank and file will follow.[23] Here is the place for evangelism, for if we win the people to Christ, they will long to be associated with kindred spirits. Wise leaders will capitalize on this urge. The rural

pastor is in an unparalleled place of leadership. If he wastes his time condemning his folk instead of guiding, he will lose his place in the sun. He must never condone sin, but he must spend his precious time with the remedy for it rather than in criticizing its victims.

The rural minister must love his people and feel for them. Lack of real sympathy for the people has led to many failures. Often a young preacher serves as a pastor while attending college or seminary. This is a healthy thing for both the church and the whole cause of God if the young preacher doesn't use the church as a meal ticket or steppingstone to a promotion. If he does pastor a church, he must work as if he would spend his entire life there. Much of his time will be taken up at school; but he must give enough time and energy to that pastorate to satisfy the needs, or die trying. No preacher, however young or old, can afford to contribute to the delinquency of a church of the living God. A part-time situation is rarely, if ever, satisfactory. Each church should be led to a full-time program of services as soon as possible.

4. An inadequate program of evangelism is a prime hindrance to the rural church. A church with an aggressive program of evangelism will make a survey and find out those who do not attend church and why. It will then make an effort to systematically meet the need. One church made a survey to ascertain why the folk were not attending, and many said, "We have never been invited." These people assumed that the church should take the initiative.[24] In cities where there are many churches and competition is keen, the unchurched are contacted often as a rule, but this is not true in the country. Some said, "The church is too far away." These people, however, were accustomed to driving six and eight miles every week to a town to purchase provisions.[25] This is no real difficulty in the open country because most of the people own cars. This argument can easily be met.

5. Rural people are individualistic. They are more independent in thought and feeling than their city cousins. However, this is not as prevalent as it once was. This individualism came out of the background of the rural folk. Originally each family kept to itself in its own home and barn and field, working out its own destiny.[26] Better roads, telephone, radio, television, and

improved transportation have added to the family fellowship with broader social contacts. Much of the former rigid individualism has faded. Traces enough of it remain, however, to prove a problem in many quarters, but we must remember that this individualism has often encouraged a rich culture of the soul which has proved invaluable for civilization. In many areas the farmer formerly had time for creative thought. In many rural sections there still remains a "primitive reverence," fortifying against fleshly distractions which destroy the people in the cities.[27]

EVANGELISTIC PROCEDURE FOR THE RURAL CHURCHES

The procedure will vary slightly with different localities in the open country just as it would in urban territory. There are, however, some things which are basic in both rural and urban evangelism. It may be well to consider the techniques which may be applied in either situation, as well as the specific methods employed in rural territory. The *Southern Baptist Program of Evangelism* deals thoroughly with those techniques which may be applied to either, and for that reason this treatment will have little to say at this point.[28]

1. The modern rural church must be a spiritual force in the community.[29] The scriptural and historical approach in the country has always been spiritual. Some would absorb the rural church in the social and economic procedure, but its field of operation is spiritual. The church anywhere can better serve the cause of the social, moral, and general welfare when it creates a spiritual atmosphere. In many communities, spiritual needs have been minimized, and better farming and physical improvements have been given priority. When the spiritual challenge is met, it always makes for full-orbed living. The way of Jesus was to "seek . . . first the kingdom of God . . . and all these things shall be added" (Matt. 6:33). Evangelism is a means toward accomplishing the spiritual goal. An awakened and purified society depends on a stirred conscience. Moral impulses must be alerted. The only factor in rural communities suited to produce such internal effect is the church. If the rural church disintegrates into a social organization, it loses its rightful place in the community, and wholesome social life may not long endure.

2. Institute an attractive program of evangelism in the rural church. An adequate program of evangelism for the rural church

will consist of two parts: perennial evangelism, and special evangelism. Evangelism for the rural areas has often been inadequate. For the most part the protracted meeting is about all the evangelism known and promoted. This program of evangelism has never been sufficient, but it met the needs in the past far better than it can today. The rural church cannot hope to prosper today without a program of perennial evangelism. Such a program has many phases.

(1) The members of the local church must be informed as to the needs for evangelism and how to reach these needs. The people may not rise up and demand information, but the pastor cannot move them without it. The pastor will give complete details on every deviation from their customs, explaining every new method to be used.[30] He will tell them why and how the methods should be employed. He will never rush them. He will give them time to think and discuss the proposals. The church will vote on the plans when the time is ripe.

The pastor may begin with the deacons. Let the deacons have a part in making the program. If they help formulate the plans, they will help sell them to the church and will assist in their execution. The pastor may bring the program before the council of evangelism, and from there take it to the church. He must be one hundred per cent for the program but must never appear over-anxious. The pastor will never act hastily nor push the church into a hasty decision. He will never give the feeling of "putting something over."[31] He may use the church bulletins, tracts, sermons, the state paper, and every means available to make sure that the people understand the plan. Informed members make excellent followers. Members, who have half-knowledge of the plan or incorrect information, may hurt the plan and the church by unwise statements.

It is not sufficient to thoroughly inform the members. An endless program of information and promotion must be prosecuted. Lead the people to attend denominational gatherings. Contact with other groups helps generate within the individual and the local church a necessary enthusiasm and concern. Lead the people to attend associational meetings and state meetings for instructions, inspiration, and fellowship. Interest must be aroused and kept alive. It is not generally the fault of the people when they are devoid of interest. It is usually an index of the leadership obtaining in the local church. The interest of the folk may be captured by a worthy motive and an absorbing challenge. This is where information enters. It requires keen understanding to get the attention of the people. If the leadership of the rural church understands rural people and has a genuine concern for them, it can arouse the interest. Understanding and concern must be permeated with a spirit of optimism.[32] When interest has been stimulated, great patience and tact must be used to develop rural talent.

(2) Institute a church council of evangelism.[33] The personnel and nature of the church council of evangelism are thoroughly set forth in the *Southern Baptist Program of Evangelism*. Everyone should study diligently the information given in this splendid book by Dr. C. E. Matthews. This council will work in any type of church without any modification.

(3) Survey the field. The census for the rural area serves the same purpose as in the city, but the plan for taking it varies widely. Co-operation with other churches in the community is strongly advised. Teams of two each should be arranged so that members of different churches will be represented on each team. If necessary the canvassers should be able to explain to the people the purpose of the census. In the rural community the teams will cover less territory because the homes are scattered over a large area, except in towns of twenty-five hundred. In the open country, each team may contact about five homes within a two-hour period. This requires a large core of workers if the canvass is to be finished in a half-day. The canvassers should be familiar with the material discussed in the *Southern Baptist Program of Evangelism*[34] or any other acceptable material. Each team must be given maps, cards, and all necessary material for securing this vital information.

(4) Install a weekly visitation program adapted to the need of that particular rural church. Lay evangelism is vital in the country. Rural evangelism is best accomplished through personal work.[35] Better roads have not eliminated the necessity for much walking in the country. Personal workers must walk across fields and climb into barns. They may even crawl along with farmers as they pick strawberries or cotton. Rural evangelism must never forget that cornfields and haylofts make good altars for prayer. The majority of rural church members have felt in

the past that personal work is the job of the minister and a few saintly souls.[36] This is a mistake. It must be corrected before an effective program of visitation evangelism can be worked out in the country. A workable program of visitation evangelism can be held in the country if it is carefully planned and executed.

(a)   Train carefully the visitors.

(b)   Guard against the loss of interest. Often the teams will begin with great enthusiasm and gradually let up. Careful attention at this point should be given by the pastor and the church council of evangelism. Evangelism cannot be built and sustained by mere enthusiasm. Love for the lost, a compulsion of Bible truth, and a realization of the dire need of the unsaved, linked to a firm dedication to evangelism, will assist the church in keeping alive the visitation program.

(c)   Evangelistic visitation should be done under the direction and co-ordination of the council of evangelism. If this policy is followed, visitation will never be sporadic. Visitation evangelism should be regular and purposeful.

(5)   Work with the public schools in the community if at all possible. In many states and communities, the pastor and local church can do much good through the local schools. The names of children not in Sunday School can be secured and such children can then be contacted. Christian pupils can invite and bring the unchurched children to Sunday School. Parents may often be reached through the interest shown in their children. The pastor will speak to the student body as often as feasible. The pastor and church leaders will attend certain functions of the school. The pastor will visit the field of practice when the boys are playing football, basketball, and other games of contest. This will show the young people that the pastor is really interested in them and their activities. The pastor and church leaders will stay in close contact with every phase of school life. In too many places, the public school is the center of life and activity of the local community. This is true because the churches in those communities have gone to sleep. This position may be recaptured by the church with proper interest and action. It will be healthy for the school, as well as multiplying the possibilities of evangelism. The church is not to meddle in the affairs of the school nor try to run the school, but it should be a close and influential ally of the school.

(6) Special evangelism. The rural church should promote at least two revivals each year, and one of them should be a simultaneous crusade if this method is used in the area. The revival meeting is familiar to most rural churches. For a long time it was about all the evangelism they knew. In some quarters it constitutes the program of evangelism. The revival has been abused possibly more in the rural areas than anywhere else. Since the techniques of rural revivals are well known, they will not be discussed further here except to encourage every church to plan, prepare for, and properly conduct at least two each year. The season for a rural revival effort is not as limited now as it was previously. Roads, lights, heating systems, and similar conditions have been modernized in the community, making revival effort possible almost any season of the year. If revival in the rural area is to be fruitful, it must be thoroughly prepared for and directed according to the best-known techniques.

3. Train adequate leadership. The pastor may know thoroughly the proper procedure of evangelism for the rural church, but unless he has a trained and dedicated group of leaders to work alongside of him, the task will not be adequately performed. He must teach courses in leadership and evangelism often. He should repeatedly in the Sunday School and in the worship services enlist members to take the courses of study. He will encourage the congregation to build larger and better units for service. He will methodically and persistently build a capable leadership. Thus the number of capable leaders will increase. The number of units will multiply. The size of the building and the amount of equipment will increase proportionately. All of these things are necessary for an effective program of evangelism in the country.

CHAPTER 12

EVANGELISM BEYOND THE DOORS OF THE CHURCH

New Testament churches were meant to be outdoor agencies as well as indoor institutions.[1] It was never the directive intent of Christ that His churches confine their activities to within a church house located at a certain street intersection. It was His plan that the churches go out after the lost (Luke 15:4). Jesus preached on the mountain (Matt. 5:1), and by the seaside (Matt. 13:1). John, the forerunner, preached in the wilderness (Matt. 3:1). Paul preached in private offices (Acts 13:7-12), aboard ship (Acts 27:10, 21, 25), and in prison (Acts 28:23-24). These early evangelists carried the Gospel to the people and did not wait for the people to come seeking the Gospel. Peter came into prominence by a great street sermon on the day of Pentecost (Acts 2). One of the greatest parables on evangelism ever given by Jesus was meant to urge His followers to "go out quickly into the streets and lanes of the city. . . . Go out into the highways and hedges, and compel them to come in" (Luke 14:21, 23). The evangelism of the New Testament churches was a roadside- (John 7:37), wellside- (John 4:13-30), seaside- (Luke 8:27-40), bedside- (Luke 8:49-56), tableside- (Luke 7:44-50), outside-the-doors- (John 4:30-45) evangelism.

THE VALUE OF EVANGELISM BEYOND THE DOORS OF THE CHURCH

1. It reaches great numbers of outsiders. Some people will never be reached by the regular worship services of the church. The great numbers of diluted and unconcerned will never be won for Christ even by the effective, concerted visitation program within the churches. Some are separated from all-over evangelistic approaches by ignorance and prejudice. Many doors and minds are locked against the regular overtures of the church. We must get to them. There are literally thousands of persons who

162

can be reached by radio or television. Many will sit in their own living room and hear a gospel service who would never dare go in person to an open church service. Attractive television and radio programs may create an interest that will unlock the human heart. The down-and-out soul may be reached by an open street service. The man who lives on skid row and who never thinks of going to church, may stumble upon salvation through an attractive street service. Hundreds of respectable folk have heard the Gospel and accepted Christ as Saviour through street services. Ninety-seven per cent of the unchurched population never attend services. Over ninety-five per cent of the evangelistic sermons are preached to only three per cent of the unchurched population. This cold fact should send the soul-winner outside the doors of his church in search of the lost sheep. The average pastor, by making three visits per day, week in and week out, will easily preach to more unchurched folk in the homes than in his pulpit on Sundays.

2. It enlists new workers.[2] To prosecute a vigorous program in highways and hedges, evangelism requires a great corps of workers. It will require workers to conduct street services, neighborhood prayer meetings, jail services, tract distribution, televangelism, radio programs, work in hospitals; to function as officers for new missions, and as workers in disintegrated areas of the community. For the average city church to meet the challenge of outside evangelism would require as many trained workers for that project alone as for the local Sunday School in the same church. It develops evangelists and creates a spirit of conquest.

3. It deepens the spiritual life of the church. These neglected folk are not as difficult to win as the gospel-hardened handful who attend the worship services occasionally. Tears in the eyes of new converts and the words of joy, which these folk freely express, tend to deepen the spiritual life of the workers. Busy Christians are growing Christians. It breaks up the stiffness and melts the spiritual chill which tends to throttle many church members. It breaks down class distinctions and creates understanding.[3]

4. It establishes new churches. When existing churches survey new areas of the city and send out workers to establish missions, it always results in new churches. These new churches

meet a vital need. People will not travel many blocks to begin attendance at church services. They will not, as a rule, cross railroad tracks and rivers to attend church. A thriving church must be placed within easy reach of all prospects or they will not respond. This type of evangelism will have three fruitful effects: it will multiply churches, it will increase the number of Christians, and it will meet the needs of an increasing population.

OPPORTUNITIES FOR EVANGELISM BEYOND THE DOORS OF THE CHURCH

1. The slums. Slum areas are not confined to the crowded cities but are frequently also found in rural sections. Often mill towns and oil fields are plagued with slums. There is hardly a city without a slum neighborhood. Poverty, insecurity, fear, and sin are prevalent among the inhabitants of the slums. Little is being done to reach them. Sporadic efforts and even the best of street services fall far short. Their philosophy of life is twisted. They have been crushed, and they feel sorry for themselves. They are filled with hatred and bitterness. They tend to blame others for their failures. They merely exist from day to day. They are easy prey for crime, and they constitute a cancer in the body of the community. The Gospel must penetrate among these people.

2. Industrial areas. Industrial areas are filled with the labor element of our nation. Few or none of them own their own homes. They live in crowded apartment houses without adequate playground facilities for the family. These people are important. What they think is important to the nation. They furnish the breeding ground for communism and other movements which are detrimental to the community.[4] The crowded industrial areas of our nation present one of the greatest challenges to evangelism beyond the doors of the church.

3. New housing areas. There has never been a time in the history of the American people when the cities were growing as rapidly as now. The increase of the population of the urban centers each year is equal to the entire population of the state of Alabama.[5] The Alabama Baptist Convention has twenty-six hundred churches. This does not mean that this many new churches should be organized each year, but it does point up the need of new churches in many urban centers. A recent

survey revealed that there is ample room for 29,949 new churches in the urban centers.[6] This figure is arrived at by the survey on the basis of the Southern Baptist norm. The national norm indicates that there is need for 28,132 new churches now. New housing areas are springing up over night in all the great cities of America. There are literally acres upon acres of beautiful homes standing now in places that were open fields only a few months ago. The churches in these cities must have a vision to answer such challenge. The percentage of the city population which dwells in the new housing areas is not known, but we do know that new churches built in these areas grow faster than the old churches in the established areas. They are often also more evangelistic due to the fact that they usually deal with younger people and young families in the vicinity.

4. The challenge of hospitals, homes for the aged, prisons, and correctional institutions, calls for painstaking evangelism outside the doors of the church. In 1956, 2,563,150 major crimes were committed in the United States. In the same year the total number arrested in cities of 2,500 and over was 2,070,794.[7] In 1953, 1,791,160 were arrested. This shows a frightening increase in the number of arrests in a three-year period. The number who are annually placed in penitentiaries, state and federal, is 188,730.[8] The actual cost of crime in 1954 according to J. Edgar Hoover was twenty billion dollars and the estimated damage to property by crime in 1956 was four hundred and forty million dollars (13.8 per cent greater than in 1955).[9] From 1950 to 1954, crime outstripped the population rate of increase four to one. The population increased five per cent while crime increased twenty per cent. In 1956, one major crime was committed in the United States for every 65 persons. The crime rate of the young people under 18 increased 7.9 per cent in 1953.[10] J. Edgar Hoover recently reported that in 1958 crime jumped an appalling eight per cent in the U. S. cities.[11] In the murder category, the report said cities of 25,000 to 50,000 and from 50,000 to 100,000 population showed a jump of eleven and ten per cent respectively. This compares to an overall rise of five per cent and an increase of three per cent in cities of a million plus. One-half of the adult criminals began their careers of crime as juvenile delinquents.

These figures frighten us, but far more important, they

should spur us to action for Christ. It is a recognized fact that the vast majority of these criminals have had no vital relation to the churches. They have not had the advantage of Sunday School and religious training. A few of them were christened into some church and still a smaller number were a bit more closely connected with the church. The churches must go out beyond their doors to reach with the Gospel the potential criminal, as well as the person in the grip of crime.

5. Unchurched millions never attend church. All over the nation in the outposts and in old established communities live millions who are oblivious to their spiritual needs and the presence of the churches. These millions are preoccupied with business and a constant round of busy, social life. These people are not criminals. They are ordinary citizens of our country. Many of them are diluted spiritually, but most of them are plain, ordinary, run-of-the-mill folk who could be reached. They, however, will never be reached by the ordinary efforts of the church.

Methods to Be Used Beyond the Doors of the Church

1. Christian good-will centers. The unbelievable numbers of unchurched who live in the slums and semi-industrial areas are being increasingly reached by good-will centers. The purpose of good-will centers is twofold: to prevent crime, and to lift up the fallen. The Christian good-will center seeks to reach the lost and to salvage lives for Christ that are on the verge of being ruined. In the light of crime tendencies, the good-will centers can meet a very definite need in evangelism. Nine-tenths of the young people who are involved in crime showed marked difficulties adjusting to normal social life before they were eleven years old.[12] Good-will centers can be hands of the churches seeking to prevent these maladjusted youths from reaching the stage of criminals. The Christian good-will center is one of evangelism's preventative methods. Many such institutions are operating in the nation. Southern Baptist churches alone operate over fifty such institutions. Some are privately operated and some are operated by the denomination. Many more than this number call themselves good-will centers, but their program of activity is not complete enough to designate them as such. Most of these organizations operate in downtown and slum areas. The Christian good-will center is the church reaching out to those who

have drifted beyond the reach of the ordinary services and activity of the church. Such good-will centers are employing many effective methods.

(1)   A day nursery for the children of working mothers who cannot afford nursery care for their children. A kindergarten is provided also for pre-school children who would otherwise be without parental care for many hours each day.

(2)   Graded Bible clubs for various groups.

(a)   Neighborhood couples' clubs function effectively. Couples are brought together for Bible study and activity at least one night each week. The activity consists of handicraft, recreation, and wholesome fun. Here they are taught how to use their spare time properly. They are also taught that there is a wholesome and harmless way of having fun. Previously they may have come to think that there is no fun apart from drinking and throwing wild parties.

(b)   Family clubs are held on Friday nights. The families meet at the center for Bible study, refreshments, and games. When people together study the Bible, eat, laugh and play, they are in an atmosphere where they can be helped to overcome the malady of sin.

(3)   Baby clinics are sponsored at least twice each month. Doctors and nurses render a noble service to the center at this point. Babies are examined, and mothers are counseled on how to care for their children. Ignorance of child care is often prevalent among these underprivileged people. All language groups and races are served.

(4)   Classes are conducted weekly for illiterate adults and teen-agers who are taught to read and write. This provides an excellent opportunity to teach them to read the Bible.

(5)   Sewing and cooking classes are held for women one day each week. This not only occupies their idle time but makes a definite and positive contribution to their way of living. It also gives the workers an opportunity to get close to the people and deal with them personally concerning their souls.

(6)   Preaching services are conducted regularly at such Christian centers. The people are continually urged to attend the neighborhood church. Most of them have had no religious background and at first feel utterly out of place in a church. The center provides worship for them until they can be brought into

the church. The good-will center in Fort Worth, Texas, located at 915 East Peach Street, directed by Mr. and Mrs. Robert Melton, has witnessed 777 conversions since its organization in 1947. The number enrolled in all of the activities of the center at this time is 1600 people, 400 of whom are Negroes.

2. Rescue missions. The rescue mission is an effective method for reaching the slums. Rescue missions differ from good-will centers as to aim. The work of rescue missions is a salvage program, while the Christian good-will centers purpose to prevent people from falling into ruin. The rescue mission often only conducts a gospel service, serves soup, and in most instances gives a place to sleep. It will follow-up the effort in soul-winning, but its activity is limited. There are many rescue missions for men throughout the country, but very few for fallen women and girls.

3. Industrial evangelism. There are several types of industrial evangelism. We shall deal briefly with only three.

(1) The shop meeting is one of the most commonly known and has been used with telling effect. These meetings have always been popular with the laborers. The meetings are brief and informal and are generally held at the luncheon period. They are practical and spiritual. The message is biblical and warm. Two or three brief prayers are interspersed with lively singing. Literature and pamphlets containing the plan of salvation are distributed. A brief message is generally brought at these services. Often commitments are made, but as a rule it is well to get commitments in follow-up visits rather than in the open service. This type of evangelistic service may be held in factories and shops, but a different procedure will be used in department stores, banks, etc. The committee of the church council of evangelism from the local church will ask the store owners or managers to permit them to assist in getting some sort of religious emphasis started. In many large stores the business day may begin with a brief, lively song service, and in some instances close with prayer. This will lift the ideals of the employees and will sustain and encourage Christian emphases and living.

(2) Moving pictures have been used effectively in industrial sections, especially if the area is hostile or prejudiced against the churches.[13] Use high quality film which not only

raises questions of moral ideals and difficulties but points to Christianity as the answer. Follow the film with a question-and-answer period. Show what Christianity has to say on the subject. After many weeks of this type of approach the period of questions and discussion may be followed by a couple of gospel songs and a brief eight- or ten-minute sermon. Soon these brief services may be followed by home-to-home, personal evangelism. Step by step lay the foundation for a solid approach to their souls.

(3) Establish churches in the industrial areas for the people who live there. One of the weaknesses of most of the methods used in industrial evangelism is that the contact leaves the interested worker suspended in mid-air. Men and women are generally contacted with a gospel service and with some sort of personal follow-up at the factory or outside the gates of the factory. But the follow-up is generally inadequate because helpful impressions are not ripened into convictions. A church right in the industrial community will meet the person in his home and relate him and his family to a permanent Christian fellowship. The primary purpose of soul-winning promoted by shop meetings, films, and special services will seldom be attained unless the individual is ultimately related to the church.

4. Open-air services. Open-air services provide one of the most productive fields for evangelism. When churches become over-institutionalized and their leadership highly specialized, they tend to overlook a most productive field, the open-air evangelistic service. Jesus never intended that the churches always remain indoors. The indoor church often multiplies meetings with less and less attendance. The indoor church frequently relaxes its efforts in the summertime and, in many instances, even goes on a vacation, closing its doors for weeks at a time. Summer is one of the greatest seasons for evangelism. Politics and athletics thrive in the open air.[14] The open air also provides a prolific opportunity for evangelism. Three types of meetings, the street service, the tent, and summer assemblies, are most suited to open-air evangelism.

(1) The informal street-meeting is one of the oldest and best-known methods. Small groups from the church may conduct a gospel service at a busy intersection, park, or town square. Begin with a brief song service. Intersperse with testimonies

followed by a warm, practical, gospel message. An invitation is generally given, and those who respond are dealt with further. The street contact is followed by a concerted effort from the church.

(2) The tent meeting is employed by churches in mill towns and unchurched areas of crowded cities. The services are held nightly during the week for two or three weeks. Often the tent services are held on Sunday evening before the time of the regular worship at the church. Tent services are informal and friendly. The sermons must be warm and searching in content and appeal. Thousands of middle-classed and underprivileged folk who never go to the regular indoor services of the churches will attend the easy and friendly services at the tent. When these people's hearts are warmed sufficiently, they will enter the church doors for further help and fellowship. The tent meeting is a splendid contact which the local church has with the unchurched population.

(3) Among the open-air evangelistic possibilities, summer assemblies are most prolific, especially for young people. Summer assemblies constitute the most noteworthy single evangelistic contribution which Southern Baptists, Methodists, Assembly of God, and other evangelicals are making to the life of young people. Large crowds of youths and adults are brought together in these district and state assemblies. They are taught Christian living, Sunday School and Training Union methods, as well as soul-winning. In the worship assemblies, which are held twice each day, the simple Gospel is preached and the young people are invited to publicly accept Christ as Saviour. Spiritual life is deepened, and the lost are converted. Those attending return to the local churches to do a superb job in Christian living and work for Christ. They inspire those who did not attend the assemblies. One of the greatest of these assemblies is the Falls Creek Baptist Assembly which is held for three weeks by Oklahoma Baptists in the Arbuckle mountains of Oklahoma. The enrollment for the three weeks averages annually twenty-one thousand. About five thousand attend each day worship, and from six thousand to seventy-five hundred attend each evening. Vast crowds of people who are not campers, but who feel the need for a spiritual lift, come from miles around each night. The total number of decisions range from twenty-five hundred to

three thousand each season. Oklahoma Baptists are greatly assisting the pastors in keeping the fires of evangelism aglow with this mighty assembly. We use the Falls Creek Assembly as an illustration of what all the states are doing. If not on as large a scale, certainly it can be said they are doing the same thing thoroughly and as effectively.

5. Radio and televangelism. Millions of the good, ordinary American citizenry already referred to may best be reached by radio and televangelism. Many never attend church. Some of them have no idea what a church looks like on the inside. They do not feel the need of the church. Many did not come out of religious backgrounds. Some are prejudiced and diluted. The best way to contact the majority of them is by radio and television. The homes in America have more television sets than automobiles. Seventy-five per cent of the households of America have TV sets, and only sixty-one per cent have automobiles.[15] Facts like these reveal the magnitude of the possibility of televangelism. Men and women will view television programs or listen to radio services who for reasons of their own would not be seen in a church. The testimonies of thousands of such people, whose hearts have been warmed and saved by means of radio and televangelism, fill the letter files of preachers and religious organizations who use the air and light waves to minister to them. Radio broadcasts and telecasts may be sponsored by the local church. But in the case of televangelism particularly, it is more effectively done by associational churches or by the denomination as a whole. An excellent example of denominational radio and televangelism effort is being demonstrated by the Radio and Television Commission of the Southern Baptist Convention. It is the fastest growing religious broadcasting group in the world.[16] It is sponsored by nine million Southern Baptists in twenty-seven states. Its radio message has been carried in forty-one languages to almost every nation in the world. It is estimated that over one hundred million people in America saw its television program in 1958.[17] Televangelism is an effort to use the mass communication medium of television to reach thousands of the unchurched. The purpose of televangelism is to use the medium of television together with the personal witness to win the lost to Christ.

The gospel message of evangelism is suited to televangelism.

It is simple, personal, and warm. It finds a ready response if it is directed to its audience by one who understands the mind of the unchurched world. The unchurched people in the television audiences are not accustomed to the type of service generally conducted in the regular worship of the church.[18] They may care little or nothing for preaching and choir music, but they will view the type of dramatic episode presented in televangelism. These episodes deal with problems that hinder a vital faith in God. The drama will present the solution. It takes the mighty truths of the New Testament and many of the parables and dresses them in modern setting and coloring. However the TV audience does not find this out until the last few seconds of the show. By this great medium of evangelism, the otherwise unapproachable have been convicted of the need of soul salvation. The letter files of Dr. Paul Stevens, head of the Radio and Television Commission of Southern Baptists, and all others who conduct programs of this nature, carry heart-warming letters. The contents of these will thrill any who are anxious to see the lost saved. Recently Dr. Stevens received a letter which told him how an entire team of basketball players in Missouri were led to hear the Baptist Hour by one of their teammates. All of them were saved and united with the church. A letter from a chaplain of a correctional institution in Florida informed Dr. Stevens, "I feel that it is my God-given duty and privilege to make this gratifying report to you pertaining to the results of the campaign in our institution. . . . We had a gratifying, but small viewing group in each dormitory day-room where the TV sets were located on the first day. Since this first program, the viewing parties' attendance has increased steadily until now almost the entire institutional population is eagerly watching our program." When televangelism is promoted and sponsored by all the churches of a given city or an entire denomination, they can produce a quality telecast as well as work out a very effective system of building an audience.

(1) Each church can promote church-wide visitations scheduled for each Sunday afternoon, directed by the televangelism committee of the church.

(2) Sunday School classes may meet for tea at the time of the telecast and invite the unchurched in the class to the telecast. The story may be discussed after the dramatic episode has

closed. Each unchurched person present will be given an episode leaflet which will contain in print the heart of the drama which he has just viewed.

(3) Neighborhood viewing groups which are sponsored by men and women from the participating churches may also invite unchurched families to their living rooms to view the televangelism program. In some cases Christian neighbors may invite their unchurched friends to come for refreshments and see the telecast with them. The worker may follow up the episode with further helps, if necessary.

(4) Neighbors and friends may merely call their unchurched neighbors and remind them to see the telecast in their own homes. The unchurched friend may not necessarily be told the purpose of the telecast. He may only be told that it is a telecast which you like and have received a blessing from, and which may, in turn, bless him.

(5) Episode leaflets may be handed out before the telecast or mailed to prospects whose names are suggested by church members. There are many ways in which Christians and their local church may co-operate to combine televangelism with personal evangelism to an effective degree.

Televangelism is the newest technique in evangelism and is possibly the most far-reaching one which we have fallen upon in recent years. It is now estimated that Southern Baptists alone in their televangelism, with the use of one hundred and three television stations, are reaching no less than twenty million people each Sunday. Lutheran televangelism which operates under the name of "This Is the Life" has been on the air for some time, and no doubt is reaching with its message a similar number of people. All interested in evangelism were keenly alerted in 1957 when Billy Graham during the New York Crusade brought the evangelistic services by TV to the American public for several Saturday nights. During this time no less than fifty thousand people were reported to have found Christ as Saviour through these televised services. It was then that we began to realize more keenly than ever the possibilities of televangelism.

6. Mission Sunday Schools and missions. These constitute our best answer to the new housing areas and other unchurched sections of our growing cities. Alert pastors and evangelistic

churches will continue to watch the growing and extending areas of the city. They will buy lots .and set up Sunday Schools in those areas which will be developed into missions and finally into churches. Reaching the new housing areas and unchurched areas may be done in two ways. In the first place, it may be done by the individual church; or it may be done in the city missions' committee. Many of the evangelical denominations have city missionaries and associational missionaries. These men work in conjunction with the pastors and churches of the given area or city in locating mission Sunday Schools and establishing churches. This will prevent the overlapping of the churches and will properly space the mission Sunday Schools so as to meet the needs of the people.

It is an established fact that new churches grow faster than the older churches, and that new churches are more evangelistic than the old established churches. In the pioneer areas of Southern Baptist work, as well as in the work of other evangelicals, it has been found that the percentage of increase in membership among these newly organized churches is far greater than the percentage of increase among the established churches in the older areas.[19] The mission Sunday School and new-church method is not only needed in new housing areas and in pioneer sections, but it is also needed in our old cities. It has been found that the population of America is no longer only shifting westward, but it is moving backwards and forwards. In this continued movement, many people have been lost to the churches. They will move from one city to another and into areas where there are no churches in easy reach, and thus become detached. They lose their effectiveness and the joy of their salvation. They soon come to mean nothing to the cause of Christ in the earth. An alert city missions program will be aware of this and work tirelessly at solving the problem.

NOTES

CHAPTER 1
Theological Basis of Evangelism

1. Charles G. Finney, *Revivals of Religion* (New Jersey: Fleming H. Revell Co.), p. 4.
2. T. A. Kantonen, *Theology of Evangelism* (Philadelphia: Muhlenburg Press, 1954), p. 3.
3. Henry Cook, *The Theology of Evangelism* (London: Carey Kingsgate Press, 1951), p. 18.
4. Kantonen, *op. cit.*, p. 8.
5. Cook, *op. cit.*, p. 23.
6. W. C. Bower, *Religion and the Good Life,* p. 142.
7. Edwin E. Aubrey, *Present Theological Tendencies* (New York: Harper & Brothers, 1936), p. 195.
8. W. B. Pillsbury, *The History of Psychology* (Ann Arbor: George Wahr, 1929), p. 297.
9. *Ibid.,* p. 297.
10. Walter Barlow, *God So Loved* (Los Angeles: Fleming H. Revell Co., 1958), p. 15.
11. Elmer G. Homrighausen, *Choose Ye This Day* (Philadelphia: Westminster Press, 1943), p. 48.
12. Fred L. Fisher, *Christianity Is Personal* (Nashville: Broadman Press, 1951), p. 53.
13. Barlow, *op. cit.*, p. 17.
14. John Dillenberger and Claud Welch, *Protestant Christianity* (New York: Charles Scribner's Sons, 1954), p. 30.
15. *Ibid.,* p. 30.
16. Fisher, *op. cit.,* p. 42.
17. *Ibid.,* p. 45.
18. *Ibid.,* p. 46.
19. *Ibid.,* p. 55.
20. *Ibid.,* p. 55.
21. Homrighausen, *op. cit.,* p. 59.
22. *Ibid.,* p. 61.
23. Barlow, *op. cit.,* p. 58.

CHAPTER 2

Biblical Background

1. George Sweazey, *Effective Evangelism* (New York: Harper & Brothers, 1953), p. 19.
2. Charles H. Spurgeon, *The Soul Winner* (New York: Fleming H. Revell Co., 1895), p. 10.
3. S. M. Zwemer, *Evangelism Today* (New York: Fleming H. Revell Co., 1944), p. 13.
4. *Ibid.*, p. 19.
5. Ambrose M. Bailey, *Evangelism in a Changing World* (New York: Round Table Press, 1936), p. 38.
6. *Ibid.*, p. 38.
7. *Ibid.*, p. 39.
8. F. D. Whitesell, *Basic New Testament Evangelism* (Grand Rapids: Zondervan Publishing Co., 1949), p. 22.
9. Charles L. Goodell, *Heralds of a Passion* (New York: George H. Doran Co., 1921), p. 15.
10. *Ibid.*, p. 16.
11. L. R. Elliot, former librarian of Southwestern Baptist Theological Seminary, Fort Worth, Texas.
12. John R. Rice, *The Soul Winner's Fire* (Chicago: The Moody Press, 1941), p. 58.
13. Gaines S. Dobbins, *Evangelism according to Christ* (Nashville: Broadman Press, 1949), p. 32.
14. *Ibid.*, p. 34.

CHAPTER 3

Dynamics of Evangelism

1. J. B. Lawrence, *The Holy Spirit in Evangelism* (Grand Rapids: Zondervan Publishing House, 1954), p. 7.
2. *Ibid.*, p. 7.
3. Griffith H. Thomas, *The Holy Spirit of God* (Grand Rapids: Eerdmans, 1955), p. 203.
4. Forsyth, "Intellectualism and Faith," *The Hibbert Journal*, Vol. XI, (January, 1913), p. 326.
5. Thomas, *op. cit.*, p. 166.
6. *Ibid.*, p. 187.
7. *Ibid.*, p. 188.
8. W. T. Conner, *The Work of the Holy Spirit* (Nashville: Broadman Press, 1949), p. 106.

9. *Ibid.*, p. 107.
10. Thomas, *op. cit.*, p. 170.
11. *Ibid.*, p. 174.
12. Conner, *op. cit.*, p. 138.
13. *Ibid.*, p. 138.

CHAPTER 4
The Evangelistic Church

1. G. Campbell Morgan, *Evangelism* (Chicago: Fleming H. Revell Co., 1904), p. 29.
2. F. D. Whitesell, *Basic New Testament Evangelism* (Grand Rapids: Zondervan Publishing House, 1949), p. 134.
3. W. L. Muncy, Jr., *A History of Evangelism in the United States* (Kansas City, Kan.: Central Seminary Press, 1945), p. 49.
4. Roy H. Short, *Evangelism through the Local Church* (Nashville: Abingdon Press, 1947), p. 15.
5. Translation from Greek by author.
6. Short, *op. cit.*, p. 23.
7. L. R. Scarborough, *With Christ After the Lost* (Nashville: Broadman Press, 1952), p. 62.
8. *Ibid.*, p. 62.
9. Whitesell, *op. cit.*, p. 136.
10. William E. Biederwolf, *Evangelism* (New York: Fleming H. Revell Company, 1921), p. 44.
11. Morgan, *op. cit.*, p. 80.
12. George E. Sweazey, *Effective Evangelism* (New York: Harper & Brothers, 1953), p. 26.

CHAPTER 5
Pastoral Evangelism

1. H. C. Weber, *Evangelism* (New York: The Macmillan Company, 1929), p. 145.
2. Translation, from Greek by Author.
3. *Ibid*, p. 145.
4. A. W. Blackwood, *Evangelism in the Home Church* (New York: Abingdon Press, 1942), p. 51. 810 Broadway, Nashville 2, Tennessee.
5. C. L. Goodell, *Pastoral and Personal Evangelism* (London: Fleming H. Revell Company, 1907), p. 21.
6. John Shearer, *Old Time Revivals* (Philadelphia: The Million Testaments Campaign, 1932), p. 3.
7. L. R. Scarborough, *With Christ After the Lost* (Nashville: Broadman Press, 1952), p. 75.

8. C. W. Brewbaker, *Evangelism and Present World-Order* (London: Fleming H. Revell Company, 1932), p. 67.
9. James Hastings, editor, *The Speaker's Bible* "Acts of the Apostles", (Edinburg: Turnbull and Spears, 1927), Vol. I, p. 75.
10. Bryan Green, *The Practice of Evangelism* (New York: Charles Scribner's Sons, 1951), p. 141.
11. G. E. Sweazey, *Effective Evangelism* (New York: Harper & Brothers, 1953), p. 205.
12. A. C. Archibald, *New Testament Evangelism* (Philadelphia: Judson Press, 1946), p. 30.
13. C. E. Matthews, *The Southern Baptist Program of Evangelism* (Nashville: Convention Press, 1956), p. 34.
14. *Ibid.*, p. 117.
15. W. E. Grindstaff, *Ways to Win* (Nashville: Broadman Press, 1957), p. 130.
16. F. L. Fagley, *Parish Evangelism* (London: Fleming H. Revell Co., 1926), p. 78.
17. L. D. Cartwright, *Evangelism for Today* (St. Louis: The Bethany Press, 1934), p. 81.

CHAPTER 6

Visitation Evangelism

1. Dawson C. Bryan, *Building Church Membership through Evangelism* (New York: Abingdon Press, 1952), p. 50.
2. Sidney M. Powell, *Where Are the People?* (New York: Abingdon-Cokesbury Press, 1942), p. 117.
3. A. Earl Kernahan, *Adventures in Visitation Evangelism* (New York: Fleming H. Revell Co., 1928), p. 13.
4. George E. Sweazey, *Effective Evangelism* (New York: Harper & Brothers, 1953), p. 97.
5. James C. Coates, "A Visitation Program for the Local Church" (Thesis, Southwestern Baptist Theological Seminary, 1957), p. 10.
6. Kernahan, *op. cit.*, p. 86.
7. *Ibid.*, p. 15.
8. *Ibid.*, p. 29.
9. W. E. Grindstaff, *Ways to Win* (Nashville: Broadman Press, 1957), p. 105.
10. R. A. Torrey, *How to Work for Christ* (New York: Fleming H. Revell Co.), p. 183.
11. L. R. Scarborough, *With Christ after the Lost* (Nashville: Broadman Press, 1952), p. 82.

12. John T. Sisemore, *The Ministry of Visitation* (Nashville: Broadman Press, 1954), p. 21.
13. Bryan, *op. cit.*, p. 51.
14. Scarborough, *op. cit.*, p. 83.
15. Sweazey, *op. cit.*, p. 106.
16. *Ibid.*, p. 113.
17. *Ibid.*, p. 113.
18. Bryan, *op. cit.*, p. 121.
19. Arthur C. Archibald, *New Testament Evangelism* (Philadelphia: The Judson Press, 1946), p. 106.
20. *Ibid.*, p. 107.

CHAPTER 7

Educational Evangelism

1. A. J. William Myers, *Educational Evangelism* (London: National Sunday School Union), p. 12.
2. H. C. Weber, *Evangelism* (New York: Macmillan Co., 1929), p. 149.
3. R. H. Short, *Evangelism through the Local Church* (New York: Abingdon Press, 1956), p. 46.
4. David M. Dawson, *More Power in Soul Winning* (Grand Rapids: Zondervan Publishing House, 1957), p. 57.
5. W. L. Muncy, Jr., *A History of Evangelism in the United States* (Kansas City, Kan.: Central Seminary Press, 1945), p. 104.
6. L. R. Scarborough, *With Christ after the Lost* (Nashville: Broadman Press, 1952), p. 67.
7. Ruby Moore, "The Sunday School a Soul-Winning Agency" (Thesis, Southwestern Baptist Theological Seminary, 1937), p. 27.
8. F. W. Hannan, *The Sunday School an Evangelistic Opportunity* (New York: The Methodist Book Concern, 1920), p. 54.
9. *Ibid.*, p. 58.
10. R. O. Feather, *Personal Work in the Sunday School and Training Union* (Unpublished work, Baptist Book Store, Fort Worth, Texas, 1957), p. 70. Used by permission.
11. George E. Sweazey, *Effective Evangelism* (New York: Harper & Brothers, 1953), p. 183.
12. J. N. Barnette, *One to Eight* (Nashville: The Sunday School Board of the Southern Baptist Convention, 1954), p. 7.
13. Feather, *op. cit.*, p. 74.

CHAPTER 8

Preparation and Performance in Revival

1. C. E. Matthews, *The Southern Baptist Program of Evangelism* (Nashville: Convention Press, 1956), p. 40.
2. George Sweeting, *The Evangelistic Campaign* (Chicago: Moody Press, 1955), p. 19.
3. *Ibid.*, p. 20.
4. *Ibid.*, p. 21.
5. Douglas V. Steere, *On Beginning from Within* (New York: Harper & Brothers, 1943).
6. F. L. Fagley, *Parish Evangelism* (London: Fleming H. Revell Co., 1926), p. 98.
7. Mr. Torrey's statement was in circulation at the time he was living, but as far as can be ascertained, it has not appeared in any of his books.
8. Arthur B. Strickland, *The Great American Revival* (Cincinnati: Standard Press, 1934), p. 45.
9. *Ibid.*, p. 87.
10. B. R. Lacy, Jr., *Revivals in the Midst of the Years* (Richmond: John Knox Press, 1943), p. 110.
11. Robert J. Wells and John R. Rice (ed.), *How to Have a Revival* (Wheaton: Sword of the Lord Publishers, 1946), p. 68.
12. G. B. F. Hallock, *The Evangelistic Cyclopedia* (New York: George H. Doran Co., 1922), p. 265.
13. L. R. Scarborough, *With Christ after the Lost* (Nashville: Broadman Press, 1952), p. 77.

CHAPTER 9

Evangelistic Invitation

1. F. D. Whitesell, *Sixty-five Ways to Give Evangelistic Invitations* (Grand Rapids: Zondervan Publishing House, 1952), p. 11.
2. L. R. Scarborough, *With Christ after the Lost* (Nashville: Broadman Press, 1952), p. 145.
3. C. B. Templeton, *Evangelism for Tomorrow* (New York: Harper & Brothers, 1957), p. 163.
4. From *Choose Ye This Day* by E. G. Homrighausen. Copyright 1943, by Westminster Press. Used by permission.
5. *Ibid.*, p. 60.
6. *Ibid.*, p. 60.
7. Scarborough, *op. cit.*, p. 146.
8. Whitesell, *op. cit.*, p. 11.

9. C. E. Matthews, *The Southern Baptist Program of Evangelism* (Nashville: Convention Press, 1956), p. 91.
10. W. E. Grindstaff, *Ways to Win* (Nashville: Broadman Press, 1957), p. 186.
11. Templeton, *op. cit.*, p. 163.
12. John Shearer, *Old Time Revivals* (Philadelphia: The Million Testaments Campaign, 1932), p. 3.
13. Templeton, *op. cit.*, p. 166.
14. G. C. Loud, *Evangelized America* (New York: Lincoln Mac Veagh, The Dial Press, 1928), p. 99. Used by permission.
15. Henry L. Burkitt, *History of the Kehukee Baptist Association* (Philadelphia: Lippincott, Grambo & Co., 1850), p. 144.
16. Whitesell, *op. cit.*, p. 16.
17. Templeton, *op. cit.*, p. 169.
18. Scarborough, *op. cit.*, p. 150.
19. John R. Rice and Robert J. Wells (ed.), *How to Have a Revival* (Wheaton: Sword of the Lord Publishers, 1946), p. 191.
20. Grindstaff, *op. cit.*, p. 191.
21. *Ibid.*, p. 193.
22. Matthews, *op. cit.*, p. 93.
23. *Ibid.*, p. 99.

CHAPTER 10
Conservation of Results

1. Translation from Greek by author.
2. L. R. Scarborough, *With Christ after the Lost* (Nashville: Broadman Press, 1952), p. 84.
3. *Ibid.*, p. 109, f.
4. W. E. Grindstaff, *Ways to Win* (Nashville: Broadman Press, 1957), p. 204.
5. George E. Sweazey, *Effective Evangelism* (New York: Harper & Brothers, 1953), p. 216.

CHAPTER 11
Rural Evangelism

1. Harry Maurice North, *The Harvest and the Reapers* (Nashville: Cokesbury Press, 1931), p. 154.
2. J. W. Jent, *Rural Church Problems* (Shawnee: Oklahoma Baptist University Press, 1935), p. 61.
3. L. R. Scarborough, *With Christ after the Lost* (Nashville: Broadman Press, 1952), p. 84.

4. *Southern Baptist Handbook, 1957* (Nashville: Convention Press), p. 31.
5. Calvin Schnucker, *How to Plan the Rural Church Program* (Philadelphia: Westminster Press, 1954), p. 97.
6. *Information Please Almanac, 1958* (New York: Macmillan Co.), p. 495.
7. Schnucker, *op. cit.*, p. 98.
8. M. T. Judy, *The Larger Parish and Group Ministry* (Nashville: Abingdon-Cokesbury Press), p. 38.
9. Schnucker, *op. cit.*, p. 98.
10. Jent, *op. cit.*, p. 104.
11. *Southern Baptist Handbook, op. cit.*, p. 36.
12. *Information Please Almanac, op. cit.*, p. 495.
13. Author arrived at this estimation believing the same percentage of unchurched, which holds across the nation, would be true of the rural areas.
14. Arthur W. Hewitt, *God's Back Pasture* (New York: Willett, Clark & Co., 1941).
15. *Southern Baptist Handbook, op. cit.*, p. 36.
16. E. D. Brunner, *Church Life in the Rural South* (New York: George H. Doran Co., 1923), p. 48.
17. U.S. Census, 1950 Special report, PE No. 5c, Fertility Table 32.
18. Rolvix Harlan, *A New Day for the Country Church* (Nashville: Abingdon-Cokesbury Press, 1925), p. 49.
19. Jent, *op. cit.*, p. 99.
20. *Ibid.*, p. 100.
21. Garland A. Bricker, *Solving the Country Church Problem* (New York: Jennings & Graham, 1913), p. 180.
22. *Ibid.*, p. 95.
23. *Ibid.*, p. 95.
24. Schnucker, *op. cit.*, p. 101.
25. *Ibid.*, p. 101.
26. North, *op. cit.*, p. 144.
27. J. O. Ashenhurst, *The Day of the Country Church* (New York: Funk and Wagnalls Co., 1910), p. 39.
28. C. E. Matthews, *The Southern Baptist Program of Evangelism* (Nashville: Convention Press, 1956), pp. 32-154.
29. Ashenhurst, *op. cit.*, p. 36.
30. L. G. Frey, *Romance of Rural Churches* (Nashville: Tennessee Convention Board, 1947), p. 69.
31. *Ibid.*, p. 69.
32. Jent, *op. cit.*, p. 62.
33. Matthews, *op. cit.*, p. 119.

34. *Ibid.,* p. 125.
35. Earl A. Roadman, *The Country Church and Its Program* (New York: Methodist Book Concern, 1925), p. 47.
36. S. G. Neil, *A Great Evangelism* (Philadelphia: Judson Press, 1929), p. 168.

CHAPTER 12

Evangelism Beyond the Doors of the Church

1. L. R. Scarborough, *With Christ after the Lost* (Nashville: Broadman Press, 1952), p. 141.
2. *Ibid.,* p. 144.
3. *Ibid.,* p. 144.
4. George E. Sweazey, *Effective Evangelism* (New York: Harper & Brothers, 1953), p. 261.
5. Letter from Dr. Courts Redford, Superintendent of Home Mission Board of the Southern Baptist Convention, March 3, 1959.
6. The preliminary state survey made under direction of Dr. S. F. Dowis in 1957.
7. *Information Please Almanac, 1958* (New York: Macmillan Co.), p. 334.
8. *World Almanac, 1958* (New York: New York World Telegram), p. 311.
9. *Fort Worth Star Telegram,* April 25, 1957.
10. *Facts on Crime* (Supplement to the Survey Bulletin), Nov. 1954.
11. *Dallas Morning News,* March 2, 1959.
12. *Facts on Crime, op. cit.*
13. Sweazey, *op. cit.,* p. 262.
14. Charles W. Brewbaker, *Evangelism and the Present World-Order* (London: Fleming H. Revell Co., 1932), p. 93.
15. *Southern Baptist Handbook, 1958* (Nashville: Convention Press), p. 70.
16. Seth Kantor, "Evangelists of the Air Waves," *Coronet Magazine,* March, 1959, p. 192.
17. *Ibid.,* p. 192.
18. Sweazey, *op. cit.,* p. 270.
19. *Southern Baptist Handbook, 1958, op. cit.,* p. 19.

CASH RECEIPT

GOLDEN GATE BAPTIST THEOLOGICAL SEMINARY

CALIFORNIA

Date __3-30__ 19__76__

Received of __Bruce Swetnam__

Paid on Account _____ $_____

Cleaning Deposit_____ $_____

Rent_____ $_____

Matriculation _____ $ _75.00_

Guest Housing_____ $_____

Other_____ $_____

Other_____ $_____

Thank You | **TOTAL** | $ _75.00_

Golden Gate Baptist Theological Seminary

26318

Per _____
MBF   For the Business Manager